# ROYAL VISITORS
## TO SUSSEX

# ROYAL VISITORS TO SUSSEX

### From 491 to 1991

## BRIGID CHAPMAN
### With illustrations by the author

**CGB CLIFFE**
Lewes, Sussex

*For Liz and Pru, with love*

First published 1991
Copyright © 1991 Brigid Chapman
and CGB CLIFFE

ISBN  1 873983 00 X

Cover design by Helen Fenton

Printed and bound by LR Printing Services Ltd
Burgess Hill, West Sussex RH15 9UA

# ROYAL VISITORS TO SUSSEX

## Contents

# ACKNOWLEDGEMENTS

IN my search for records of royal visits I have been greatly helped by Mrs Joyce Crow, librarian of the Sussex Archeological Society, and her colleagues, who took endless trouble tracking down reliable accounts of royal occasions. I am also deeply indebted to Miss Vera Hodsell and the staff of the Lewes branch of East Sussex County Library and to the officers and members of local history societies in East and West Sussex. And many thanks too to all the newspaper reporters who were on the spot when the kings and queens, princes and princesses, came to the county and who recorded for posterity what they did, what they said and what they wore. . .

For advice and a great deal of practical help in the production of this book I am deeply indebted to Joyce Chester, Tony Goring, Judy Moore and Lyn Whitley - the order is alphabetical, you were all marvellous.

# INTRODUCTION

RARELY a month goes by without a member of the present royal family visiting somewhere in Sussex. In July the queen is usually at Goodwood for the races, staying at Goodwood House as the guest of the Duke of Richmond and Gordon, and keeping up with affairs of state by holding Privy Councils in the Tapestry Drawing Room. The Duke of Edinburgh, in his polo playing days, was often at Cowdray Park and now he drives, rather than rides for sport, he competes in the annual Brighton Horse Driving Trials at Stanmer Park when official engagements permit. Prince Charles has continued the polo at Cowdray tradition and he made his debut as a flat race rider at Plumpton in 1980.

Other members of the royal family make private visits to friends. Princess Margaret quite recently surprised Lewes antique dealers, much in the way her grandmother Queen Mary used to do, by turning up unannounced at a local antiques centre one Saturday afternoon. . . and guests at the wedding of Sarah Yorke and Richard Warburton found the Duke and Duchess of York and Prince Edward were in the congregation.

Then there are all the official visits - those formal occasions when tapes are cut, trees are planted, civic projects named and plaques unveiled.

Sussex people, wishing to rub shoulders with royalty - or get as close as protocol and security measures permit - know that the South of England Show at Ardingly is a good place to be. The queen has been there twice, Prince Philip was president of the show society in 1979 and dined at the showground; the Queen Mother has cast a knowledgeable eye over the sheep and cattle; the Prince of Wales has spent a day there and so has Prince Michael of Kent. Royal guest of honour in June 1990, was the Duchess of York in her capacity as president of the Hackney Horse Society, which was celebrating its centenary that year.

But royal visits have not always been so pleasant. Svein the Dane, with his thirteen year old son, Canute, came to the Bosham area in 1007 to raid and pillage and William of Normandy beat Harold of England at Hastings to become this country's first and only conqueror.

Medieval monarchs came for the hunting - and the odd siege. The first to do something really constructive for the county was Edward I who personally ordered and supervised the rebuilding of Winchelsea from around 1275. His son, when Prince of Wales, kept a stud of horses at Ditchling, and his grandson, Edward III, sailed from Winchelsea to defeat the Spaniards in 1350.

Young Edward VI brought so many people with him when he came on a progress in 1552 that there was not enough fodder for the horses and the numbers had to be drastically reduced. Elizabeth I was more considerate but, even so, the five days she and her court spent at Cowdray must have cost her host, Sir Anthony Browne, a small fortune.

The flight of Charles II, who took ship from Shoreham in 1651, brought a bit of excitement - at no cost to the county - but it was members of the House of Hanover who turned out to be its greatest benefactors.

Would Brighthelmstone have ever become Brighton, Queen of the Watering Places, were it not for George, Prince of Wales, later Regent and ultimately George IV? Would Worthing have so quickly become bigger than Broadwater, which is soon engulfed, had Princess Amelia not stayed there for her health? St Leonards no doubt benefitted considerably when the young Princess Victoria and her mother holidayed there, even though their carriage overturned and they could have been seriously hurt.

History happened here. It is the rich history of England, full of pageantry and informal fun, chicanery and honest administration, scandalous behaviour and royal righteousness. It began a long time ago. . .

# 1

# INVASION YEARS

## The Vikings and the Normans

KINGS and queens, princes and princesses have been coming to
Sussex for various reasons since the Roman legions marched
away. Not all were welcome. Early arrivals, Aelle and Cyssa, did
little to endear themselves to the people in the Pevensey area in
491 AD when, according to the *Anglo-Saxon Chronicles*, they
besieged the Roman fort of Anderida 'and killed all who were
inside, so there was not one Briton left.'

Another monarch with mayhem in mind was Svein Forkbeard,
King of Denmark who, accompanied by his thirteen year old son
Cnut, or Canute, ravaged and pillaged his way along the south
coast in 1007. So successful were these repeated raids by the
Danes on all parts of the country that Svein was virtually king of
England as well as of Denmark when he died in 1014.

His son, Canute, carried on the campaign with cruel vigour. He
returned the hostages Svein had left in his charge with their
hands, ears and noses cut off and at the same time demanded
£21,000 in tribute. Two years later, at the age of twenty three, he
became the first Danish king of all England and in his seventeen
year reign he proved to be a gifted and able leader, atoning for his
early acts of cruelty by re-building war damaged churches, giving
lavishly to religious houses, and travelling to Rome to visit its
holy shrines.

There is a tradition in Bosham, a sea port since Roman times,
that this paragon of kingly virtues lived there with his wife,
Emma, and that his little daughter is buried in the church.
Bosham, like Southampton and a number of other seaside
settlements, also claims to be the place where King Canute
demonstrated to his flattering courtiers that royal authority does
not extend to mastery of the sea.

Henry of Huntingdon (1084-1155) describes in detail what occurred on that occasion but does not say where it happened. He writes of Canute: 'His courtiers vied with each other in flattering him in the highest degree as the greatest of kings and the most powerful of lords - that the powers of earth, sea and sky were at his feet, and that he had but to speak to be obeyed. "Place my throne upon the seashore," he said. Then he spoke in a loud voice, and bade the waves retire and know their supreme master; but the tide kept rolling in, and dashed upon his feet and royal robes. Then said Canute to his flatterers: "Empty and worthless is the power of kings; there is but one King, He whom heaven and earth and sea obey, the King of kings and Lord of lords." And, taking his crown from his head, he sent it to the cathedral at Winchester, where it was placed upon the crown of thorns, in tribute and in token of submissive loyalty to his Maker, and he never wore it any more.'

The archeological and anti-quarian interests of three vicars of Bosham have a lot to do with the Canute tradition becoming so established in local folklore that it is generally accepted as fact. In the church there is a col-oured tile of a Danish raven above what is claimed to be Canute's little daughter's last resting place, as well as a memorial plaque put up by the children of the parish in 1906.

The Rev Henry Mitchell was the first vicar of Holy Trinity, Bosham, to do some-thing positive about substan-tiating the 'buried daughter' tradition. In August 1856 he persuaded stonemasons working in the church to investigate the spot at the east end of the nave where he had been told the child's coffin lay. Among his informants, he says in a paper about his excavations published in the *Sussex Archeological Collections* of that year, was the Rev William Kilwick, vicar of Bosham from 1800 until his death in 1838, as well as a Mr Harris and 'Mr Hay, the Historian of Chichester.'

He must have been overjoyed when the iron bar wielded by one of the workmen struck on stone and a coffin 5ft long was revealed. When it was opened, the lid being broken into two pieces in the process, it was found to contain the remains of a skeleton measuring 3ft 9ins but with no ornaments or any vestige of clothing.

Among the witnesses to the disinterment were Mr C Sturges Jones, a surgeon from Chichester and the artist, Edgar Varley who 'at once made a most correct and careful drawing' of the three to five inch stone coffin. For a few weeks the coffin and its tragic contents - the little girl was said to have drowned, aged about eight, in the Manor House moat - was on show to visitors, then it was resealed and reburied. Mr Mitchell had no doubt that he had confirmed the Canute connection with Bosham, and in his paper, points out that it was an ideal place for the king to communicate with his overseas interests. 'Accordingly, he occasionally occupied the old Roman palace at Stone Wall, and during one of his stays there, with Emma his queen, lost the child, whose remains have now been discovered,' he writes.

Another incumbent, the Rev Kenneth MacDermott, added to the legend. In *Bosham Church: Its History and Antiquities,* published by subscription in 1911, he not only has King Canute living at the Manor House rather than at Stone Wall, the Roman villa built by Vespasian, but suggests that he rebuilt the church under the nave of which 'a daughter of his lies buried.'

In 1954, when the nave of the church was being repaired, another old stone coffin was discovered near the chancel steps, not far from the little girl's grave. It contained the arthritic bones of a powerfully built man of about sixty and immediately people remembered another local tradition - that Earl Godwin, who virtually ruled over the whole of the south of England in the first half of the eleventh century, was also buried at Bosham, the manor of which he held. He had died of apoplexy in 1053 while dining with his son-in-law, Edward the Confessor, at Winchester and was buried, according to the *Chronicles,* 'within the Old Minster.'

In the spring of 1981 two burials in charcoal, a custom practised from the ninth to the twelfth centuries, were discovered in the chapel crypt. As yet no local legends have cropped up to account for them . . .

A ROYAL visitor about whom there is no doubt is William, Duke of Normandy. He came in anger to claim the kingdom he had been promised by Edward the Confessor, but which had instead been given by the Parliament of the day, the Witanagemot, to Harold, son of Earl Godwin.

The *Bayeux Tapestry,* a record in needlework attributed to William's wife, Matilda, and her ladies, gives the Norman version of the Conquest and the events leading up to it. Harold is seen setting sail in 1064 from his manor of Bosham to convey the promise of the succession to William and is also shown swearing an oath of loyalty to him. So when Harold had himself crowned in the new abbey of West Minster on January 6, the day after King Edward died, William had cause to be more than a little annoyed.

He at once made plans to invade England and his claim his inheritance. He sent to Rome for the Pope's blessing on the project and spent the next six months building ships and gathering an army together. On September 27, 1066 he set off from St Valery-sur-Somme with his cavalry and infantry - the *Bayeux Tapestry* shows almost as many horses as riders in the invasion fleet - bound for the coast of Sussex.

He landed with some 9,000 troops at Pevensey on Michaelmas Eve, having lost only two ships on the calm Channel crossing, and immediately fell flat on his face. The *Chronicle of Battel Abbey*

Panels from the Bayeux Tapestry show Harold at a farewell feast before embarking from Bosham. A barefoot follower carries one of his hunting dogs aboard. Below, William of Normandy's cavalry crossing a calm Channel to invade England.

records the incident: 'It happened as the duke left his ship, that he fell upon his face, making his nose somewhat bloody upon the beach, and grasping the earth with his outstretched hands.'

After this undignified descent onto Sussex soil William stayed long enough at Pevensey to built a wooden fort inside the massive stone walls of the stronghold built by the Romans before moving along the coast to Hastings, where there was a better anchorage.

He set up his headquarters on the clifftop at West Hill, putting up another wooden castle which he had brought over in sections from Normandy, and surrounding it with protective earthworks. From here, on October 14, 1066 he marched six miles north towards London and found his way blocked by the Saxons.

Harold was at York celebrating his victory at Stamford Bridge over Harold Hardrada, a Norwegian claimant to the throne he had seized, when he heard of William's arrival at Pevensey. He came quickly to London to muster new men-at-arms and marched towards Hastings. Historians disagree about whether he planned to press on to the coast or decided to take up a defensive position at Caldbec Hill to stop the Normans' advance on London. Whatever the reason on the morning of October 14 Harold deployed his army on the slopes above the Senlac stream, a site now occupied by the Battle Abbey estate, and William lined up his Norman, Breton and Flemish troops on the opposite slope of Telham Hill.

The sun rose at 6.22am that day but it was not until 9am that the slaughter started. The Norman foot soldiers, in chain mail and backed by a cavalry of some 3,000 heavily armoured knights, attacked with sword and lance and the Saxons responded with axe blows that sliced through armour like butter.

William had three horses killed under him as the Normans repeatedly tried to breach the Saxon shield wall. Attack after attack was repulsed but the Saxon line eventually began to crumble under cavalry charges on its flanks. The end came quickly. The Normans, who had sent to Pevensey for more arrows, shot them high into the air so they rained down on the Saxons grouped round their king.

A panel of the *Bayeux Tapestry* shows the shields of the Saxons bristling with arrows and one man falling to the ground with an arrow in his head. The next scene in the embroidery is captioned 'Harold Rex Interfectus Est' and shows the king being killed by a sword thrust from a Norman horseman.

The *Anglo Saxon Chronicles* say little about the actual battle

other than that 'there were many killed on both sides' and that William returned to Hastings 'and waited there to see whether men would submit to him.'

When he found that none did, he stayed only long enough in Sussex to receive reinforcements for his army from Normandy before marching first to Canterbury and then on to London where he was crowned King of England on Christmas Day.

He left behind him, in this county of the Conquest, a permanent reminder of his visit. Battle Abbey, and the town that now surrounds it, owe their existence to William's vow 'that upon this place of battle I will found a suitable free monastery.' But some time passed before he did anything about doing so in spite of repeated reminders from the monk, William Faber, who was with him when the oath was made.

When he did give the necessary instructions for some monks to be brought over from Marmoutier to found the Abbey of St Martin there was a dispute about the site. The monks felt that the spot where Harold fell was too far away from a supply of fresh water and they wanted to build the abbey lower down on the western slope of Senlac Hill, But William insisted that it must be built on the place of his victory, regardless of water supply difficulties.

'I will so amply provide for this place, that wine shall be more abundant here than water is in any other great abbey,' he promised. He also ordered that only bread fit for a king should be served in the refectory. The monks were to have a daily allowance of thirty six ounces of Simenel or Simnel loaves made of the finest wheaten flour. These were only eaten on Simnel Sunday - the fourth in Lent - in other religious houses.

WILLIAM died in Normandy in 1087, long before the abbey was finished. It was his son, William Rufus, who in February 1094 became the first of many monarchs to perform an opening ceremony in Sussex.

'Surrounded by a huge crowd of barons and common people' he rode over from Hastings where he was waiting with his army for favourable winds to cross the Channel and invade Normandy. The abbey was dedicated with much medieval pomp and ceremony to 'the Holy and Undivided Trinity, the blessed Mary, ever Virgin, and Christ's Confessor, St Martin' and the king, bishops and barons had a great banquet afterwards.

This was not William's first visit to the county. Shortly after his accession he had to deal with a group of disgruntled Normans led by Odo of Bayeux, who had set up his headquarters with his brother, Robert de Mortain, at Pevensey Castle. William laid siege to the stronghold his father had fortified and captured it in six weeks.

Another Sussex castle he called on, this time socially rather than punitively, was Arundel. On one of his return trips from Normandy he celebrated Easter there as the guest of Earl Robert de Belleme, but just how welcome a visitor he was it is hard to say. He had the reputation of travelling around the country with an entourage of followers who behaved appallingly.

'They lived everywhere at free quarters, they trampled under foot the bread they did not eat, they washed their horses feet in good, home-brewed ale, and now and then, out of mere drunken frolic, they burnt down the house that had given them shelter for the night' writes Professor J M D Meiklejohn in his *New History of England and Great Britain.* The Anglo Saxon Chronicles say much the same thing: 'His court, in the shire where they were, did more harm than ever a court or any army should do in a peaceful land.'

THE county's next royal visitor, also to Arundel, was William's brother, Henry I, who had usurped the throne in 1100 before his elder brother, Robert, who had more right to it, could get back from a Crusade.

Henry came with an army in 1102 with the intention of teaching Robert de Belleme a lesson for leading a revolt of the barons against him. He besieged Arundel Castle, but when he found he could not win it, he left his siege engines in place and went to Bridgenorth to besiege another of de Belleme's strongholds. This one fell to him and de Belleme was attainted and deprived of all his English possessions.

King Henry was back again twelve years later. He had intended to take ship for France from Portsmouth but was prevented from doing so by the bad weather. Almost the whole year had been a disaster, meteorologically speaking. The *Chronicles* report that in May a rare star with a long beam of light shone for many nights. This caused 'so great an ebb tide that no one remembered the like before it - it was such that men went riding and walking over the Thames east of London Bridge'. There were great winds in October and an even greater gale on November 18 'and that was seen everywhere in the woods and villages afterwards.'

For seven days Henry was storm-bound in Sussex so he settled down to administer the affairs of state from Stanstead, near Westbourne, one of de Belleme's estates that had come to the crown. From there, on September 15, he ordered the Archbishop of Canterbury, to bless Ernulf, Abbot of Peterborough, as Bishop of Rochester 'whether he liked it or not.' He had called the abbot to Stanstead and offered him the bishopric but the gentle, modest monk had done his best to decline the honour.

Henry, in his will, left all de Belleme's Sussex estates, including Arundel Castle, to his widow, Queen Adeliza, who he had married two years after the death of his first wife, Maud the Good. Soon it was to be a centre of conflict again.

THE new king, Stephen, son of William the Conqueror's eldest daughter, Adela, was opposed by a rival claimant to the throne, Matilda, Henry's only child. On September 30, 1139, accompanied by her half brother, Robert of Gloucester, and 140 knights she arrived at Arundel and asked Queen Adeliza, now the wife of William d'Aubigny, third Earl of Arundel, for sanctuary and support.

Adeliza was no wicked stepmother. She had been a good friend to Matilda for many years, taking her side when, at the age of twenty six she was forced into a loveless marriage with fifteen year old Geoffrey the Fair, Count of Anjou. Again she came to her stepdaughter's aid and ordered the drawbridge to be dropped.

As soon as Matilda was safely inside Robert of Gloucester left with twelve companions to make his way to Bristol. Stephen tried to intercept him but failed, and he returned to Arundel with the intention of laying siege to the castle. He was advised against this course of action by his brother, Henry, Bishop of Winchester. 'You will find yourself fighting on two fronts,' he was told, so he allowed Matilda to join Robert at Bristol, and even provided her with an escort for the journey.

This was not a good move on Stephen's part. The West Country barons rallied to Matilda's cause and were joined by other nobles from all parts of the country. It was the beginning of eight years of civil strife and eight years of anarchy. The barons built castles as fast as they could, to defend their territories from the armies of mercenaries employed by Stephen and Matilda as they tussled for the throne. The mercenaries pillaged the countryside to get food and goods in payment for their services, and Sussex was not spared from the famine and disease that followed their locust-like looting for, in 1148, Stephen brought his troops to Pevensey to besiege the castle, then owned by Gilbert le Clare, Earl of Hertford, who had rebelled against him. He captured it and gave it to his son, Eustace.

Five years later Eustace died, campaigning in Cambridgeshire in support of his father. Stephen, from Lewes, where he was staying at the Cluniac priory of St Pancras, did some small favour to the county by confirming a grant his son had made, releasing from all civil dues lands at Pevensey which had been given to the priory by Robert de Horstede.

# 2

# MONARCHS ON THE MOVE

## The Plantagenets

MATILDA'S eldest son, Henry, succeeded where his mother had failed. When Stephen died at Dover in 1154 Henry, at the age of twenty one, became the first of England's Plantaganet kings and immediately set about restoring law and order. He pulled down 1,100 of the castles the warring nobles had put up, disbanded the troops of mercenaries, and appointed judges to travel the country to deal with the grievances of the people.

By 1179 King Henry II had his English kingdom under reasonable control and on July 9, according to the *Chronicle of Benedict of Peterborough*, he went to Portsmouth intending to cross to Normandy. But the wind was unfavourable so, accompanied by a number of bishops and nobles, he did what his grandfather had done in similiar circumstances and stayed at Stanstead.

The time he spent in Sussex was not exactly a holiday for him. On July 12 came news from France that the papal legate was rapidly losing his patience at Henry's refusal to sanction the marriage of his son, Richard, to Alice, daughter of the French king, and was threatening to put the kingdom under an interdict. Henry asked the clerics who were with him at Stanstead to appeal to the Pope against the legate in the hope of preventing the marriage and keeping Alice for himself. She was constantly in his care and his company, and there was all sorts of gossip in the court about their relationship.

On the same day he signed a charter confirming an agreement between Arnulf, Bishop of Lisieux, and Bartholomew, Bishop of Exeter, concerning the royal chaplaincy of Bosham. Another document the king issued from Stanstead granted permission to the Jews to have a cemetery outside the walls of every city.

In all Henry spent eight nights at Stanstead, then the property of the son of his old friend, William d'Aubigny, Earl of Arundel. No doubt he enjoyed the hunting and the hawking there until an old wound caused by the kick of a horse gave him trouble and he had to go to Winchester to have it treated.

It was the sporting potential of the area, as well as its proximity to Portsmouth, from where he crossed frequently to visit his French possesions, that made him decide to build a hunting lodge at Stanstead. When it was ready he sent his favourite falconers, Richard and Ralph, to the new lodge and in 1181 he appointed one named Silvester to look after his birds in the park. As well as staffing his property the king also enlarged it. He built on a room at a cost of l5s. 5d., then a kitchen for 14s. 9d. and spent 6s. 10d. on general repairs.

But how many times, if at all, he came back to hunt at Stanstead in the remaining ten years of his  reign is a matter of conjecture.  He was more often in France than in England, and when he was here it was usually only for short periods, during which he had to attend to matters of state that required nearly all his time and attention.

RICHARD the Lionheart, the subject of many a bold Crusading legend, succeeded his father in 1189. He was so busy settling scores with Saladin in the Holy Land that he was hardly ever in England until 1194, when he went through a second crowning ceremony at Westminster on April 17.

Five days later he was off to France. His army was assembled at Portsmouth, waiting to cross the Channel and subdue Philip of Aquitaine, but again there were adverse winds so Richard, like most medieval monarchs with a few days to spare from campaigning or crusading, went hunting.

But he only managed to get a day or two after the deer and wild boar at Stanstead before having to return to Portsmouth to pacify his troops. They had become tired of waiting to fight the French and had started to fight each other.

When Richard was fatally wounded by an arrow while besieging the castle of Chalus in some minor disagreement with its owner about treasure trove he was succeeded by his brother, John, the fifth and youngest son of Henry 11 and Eleanor of Aquitaine.

JOHN, after being invested in Rouen as Duke of Normandy, crossed from France to Shoreham on May 25, accompanied only by his personal entourage, and two days later he was crowned king at Westminster Abbey.

On June 16 he was back at Shoreham with a large army provided by the earls and barons of England and, after a few days of planning and preparation, set sail for France to attack King

Philip II for supporting the cause of Prince Arthur, son of an elder brother of King Richard, and a rival claimant for the crown of England. With him went William de Braose, Lord of Bramber, at that time one of his friends and most enthusiastic followers.

His campaigns in France kept John out of England in the early years of his reign. But he made a few short visits. He slipped over in 1200 for the coronation of his child bride, twelve year old Isabella of Angouleme  - and at the same time went to Battle Abbey to give the church of St Martin 'a certain small piece of the sepulchre of our Lord' which had been brought back from Palestine with other relics by his brother, Richard.

It was not until 1205 that he began to visit Sussex frequently for a) the hunting and b) to keep the Cinque Ports up to the mark about the provision of ships. Having lost Normandy he needed a navy to protect his English kingdom from invasion and looked to Hastings, Romney, Hythe, Dover and Sandwich to provide one.

This confederacy of five towns, to which had been added Rye and Winchelsea, and later 'limbs' such as Seaford, had been set up by that efficient administrator, William 1. In return for certain constitutional and commercial privileges the Cinque Ports had to supply, at their own expense, fifty seven ships for fifteen days service a year to king and country.

John also kept the royal yacht on the south coast. It was faster

The arms of the Cinque Ports showing the lions of England and the stern section of a ship of the 14th century.

and longer than the average galley and carried a crew of sixty. The Exchequer had to pay out £7 10s. every time the king used it to cross the Channel, instead of the twenty five to forty five shillings for which an ordinary galley could be chartered.

The king was at Lewes from February 24 to 28, staying either with the Cluniac monks at the Priory of St Pancras or the Benedictines at South Malling. He may well have decided to leave London because of the weather. It had been a terrible winter. The rivers had frozen and it was possible to cross the Thames on foot, and the ground was so hard that it could not be ploughed from the Feast of Circumsion on January 1 to the Feast of the Annunciation on March 25. 'A great famine arose throughout England so that one mark was paid for a bushel of corn which in Henry 11's time had cost 12d.' say the *Chronicles*.

On April 3, 1206 John was again the guest of the monks of Battle Abbey, staying with them for his usual three days. He was hospitably entertained and, to show his appreciation, he gave 'a fair vestment or casula' to Abbot John de Duvra for the high altar.

From Battle he rode the twenty two miles to South Malling, and spent the night of April 7 there before joining his friend de Braose, first at Knepp Castle and then at Arundel.

From Knepp, where he had gone to hunt, he sent an order to Alan Young of Shoreham, Walter Scott Vincent of Hastings, Wimund of Winchelsea and other barons of the Cinque Ports to 'arrest all ships they shall find at sea.' He wanted them for yet another campaign on the Continent.

The trouble that had been brewing between Church and State about the appointment of a successor to Hubert Walter as Archbishop of Canterbury finally boiled over in 1208 when, on March 23, the Pope put England under an interdict. All church services were suspended, the dead were buried without priest or prayer in unconsecrated ground, and there were no church weddings or baptisms.

Shortly before the Easter of the interdict the king made another of his mini-tours of Sussex, this time around the Chichester area, bringing a personal form of government to the people by making quite sure that his laws were being enforced and his appointed officials were carrying out their duties to the letter.

He visited the port of Pagham on March 27 and rode on to Bishop's Palace at Aldingbourne, where he stayed for three nights, before travelling the thirty six miles to Southampton. At Aldingbourne, on the day before Palm Sunday, Gervase, the sacristan of Reading, presented the king with six books of the Bible, perhaps to remind him of his religious duties.

It did not seem to have had the desired effect, for on April 6 John was authorising payment of £3   10s.   2d. to Ralph de Cornhill for the two casks of wine which had been imported at Pagham from the South of France and drunk by his household on Maundy Thursday and Good Friday.

While he was playing a waiting game with the Pope, the king had to take action against some of his English barons, including his friend de Braose, who was refusing to pay fines levied on his estates in Ireland. In an attempt to bring him to heel and secure his future loyalty John tried to get him to surrender his children into royal care. But in answer to this request Matilda, de Braose's wife, replied that she would not entrust her children to a king who was believed to have murdered his own nephew - a reference to the suspicious death of Prince Arthur, about which Shakespeare wrote so powerfully in his play: *The Life and Death of King John*.

Matilda did not wait for the king's reaction to her refusal to surrender her children to him. She fled with them to Ireland and her husband took horse and ship for France where he remained until his death. John seized the barony and castle of Bramber and gave them to his second son, the Earl of Cornwall.

With Bramber he acquired Knepp Castle, and in the ensuing years he went there several times for the hunting and shooting, staying his usual three days, and took a great interest in the administration of the estate. His liking for Knepp was shared by his young queen, Isabella, who spent the Christmas of 1214/15 there, staying for a full eleven days.

Many of King John's instruction to his agent, Roland Bloett, concerning the pursuit and the culling of the deer at Knepp,

Knepp Castle as it is today, nearly 800 years after King John ordered it to be 'burnt and destroyed' to keep it from the barons.

survive. On September 5, 1212 he wrote from Durham commanding Bloett to let Michael de Puning 'take all the fat deer he can find without the park at Knepp; as well as by bow, by his dogs; and that you cause them to be salted; and act for our advantage, as well concerning their flesh as their skins.'

On June 1, 1213 he sent 'three huntsmen with horses and sixty six dogs to hunt in the forest of Knepp' and on December 28 he sent 114 hounds and five greyhounds to hunt deer. He needed all the meat the estate could provide to feed his army which was at Dover, guarding the Gateway of England against the feared invasion from France.

The Exchequer was ordered to pay Bloett's bills for the wages of the huntsmen and carpenters, and for repair work 'in keeping, strengthening and repairing our castles of Bramber and Knepp.'

The royal wine bill was also settled, for the accounts show that Bloett was not only paid for carrying timber from St Leonards Forest to the sea but for 'enclosing our park at Knepp, in repairing the stewpond, according to our order; and for eighteen casks of wine, bought for our service.'

John was last at Knepp Castle in January, 1215, while his rebellious barons were in London working on Magna Carta. The hunting must have been particularly good because he spent four whole days there before moving on to Stanstead from where, on January 25, he directed the sheriff of Sussex to pay thirty shillings to Simon Eynulf for a cask of wine 'drunk at our house in Aldingbourne on Sunday, the Feast of the Conversion of St Paul.'

The king's inability to stay in the same place for more than a few days at a time was one of the many things about him that annoyed the barons. The Court of Common Pleas had to travel with him, which caused great inconvenience to the plaintiffs and their witnesses, so a clause was inserted in Magna Carta - 'that the Common Pleas should not follow the court of the king, but be held in a fixed place.'

A fine example of the king's mobility, and the good condition of the roads of Sussex in those days, are his journeys in the week of April 24-30, 1213. Philip of France had an army of 15,000 men and a fleet of ships ready to invade England to save its soul and bring it back into the Church of Rome. But he hesitated to launch an attack as John had mustered his own army and had fleets of ships guarding most of the Channel ports.

His soldiers and sailors needed some royal encouragement and the king delivered it personally. On April 24 he rode the thirty six miles from Arundel to Lewes; the next day the twenty two miles from Lewes to Battle; and on April 26 the forty one miles from Battle to Dover. He left Dover on April 27 to ride to Rye and then on to Winchelsea, a total of thirty miles miles or so, and there he stayed for the inevitable three days.

When a medieval monarch moved about his kingdom almost his entire household came too. As well as the bishops and barons, officers of state, the heralds, chamberlains, stewards, clerks and every sort of servant, came tables, chairs, cooking pots and often the royal bed. The cost of carrying the King John's effects around the county was borne by the Exchequer. Seven carts, hired at a daily rate of 5s. 10d. were needed to carry his weapons from

Arundel to Lewes; six two horse powered carts costing a total of thirty shillings took his goods back from Lewes to Arundel; and five shillings was paid out for another cart, also with two horses, for a journey from Chichester to Arundel, perhaps to collect some baggage that had been left behind.

Magna Carta was signed at Runnymede on June 15, 1215 but the king did not abide by many of its conditions. Instead he went marauding north with an army of mercenaries to deal with Alexander 11, King of the Scots. On this campaign he developed the nasty habit of setting fire with his own hand to the house in which he had spent the night, something that fortunately he never did in Sussex.

While he was in Scotland Philip of France sent his son, Louis, to seize England and at first he was welcomed by the barons but even with their help he was unable to take Dover Castle. Louis landed on the Isle of Thanet on May 14. John was in Canterbury a week later and at the Cinque Port 'limb' of Seaford checking on his ships on May 23 and 24. He then went to Bramber where he stayed his regulation three days before leaving Sussex for the last time. A month later he ordered the castle of Knepp to be 'burnt and destroyed' to prevent it falling into the hands of the barons, and gave similar instructions in respect of the Norman castles of Hastings and Pevensey

On October 19, 1216 John died in Newark Castle - from dysentery brought on by too many peaches combined with too much new cider. On the way there someone in his service misjudged the tides in the Wellstream estuary and the pack animals, the goods they carried, and several members of the royal household were lost in the Wash.

PRINCE Henry, John's eldest son, was only nine when he was crowned, and until he came of age he did not have much say in the government of the country. And he was not the best of rulers when he did. He came to Sussex on two occasions, first in the ninth year of his reign when he was received with much splendour by Henry Hussey at his manor house at Harting. The king was then on his way from Bosham, where he had disembarked on his return from France, to Winchester.

It was King Henry III's second visit that had repercussions on the whole fabric of political life. Before 1264, when his army was defeated at Lewes by Simon de Montfort and the barons, the people had virtually no say in the government of the country. Kings and queens, barons and bishops, and frequently the Pope and his cardinals, had imposed whatever taxes and laws they liked - and felt they could get away with.

After his defeat Henry was forced to sign the Mise of Lewes, an agreement between the himself and the barons appointing twenty three peers, eleven bishops, 105 clerics, two knights from every shire and two citizens from each important town, including the Cinque Ports, to meet at Westminster and form a Parliament with a House of Commons, of a sort, and a House of Lords. It was the beginning of parliamentary democracy.

But in the spring of 1264 there seemed little likelihood that the monarchy would be forced to accept some control of its absolute authority. There had been trouble for some time between the barons and the king, much of it due to Henry's inability to keep his word. He repeatedly promised to abide by Magna Carta and repeatedly failed to do so. He was greedy and he was profligate. He taxed London and the large towns heavily and much of the gold he extorted he gave to the papal legate Cardinal Otho, who, it was said, drained England of more money than he left in it.

The last straw came when Henry accepted Pope Innocent's offer of the crown of Sicily for his son, Edmund, and pledged England to repay the cost of taking that island by force of arms. The barons and the people, however, insisted that the wealth of the land belonged not to the king, to do as he wished with, but to the whole nation, and for this principle they were prepared to fight.

De Montfort and the barons were in London when Henry, determined to exert his authority, raised his red dragon standard at Oxford and marched on Northampton, capturing the castle there easily and going on to mop up other pockets of resistance in the Midlands. The rival leaders then tried to outwit each other by jinking with their followers round the country. De Montfort was strong in London and Dover but Henry, who had hopes of support from the Cinque Ports, skirted the capital and made his way through the Weald to the coast.

Many men died when the king came to Sussex for the second time and not all of them on the battlefield at Lewes. First to fall was the royal cook, Thomas, who was shot by 'a certain countryman' as he rode well ahead of the armed column as it passed the convent of Combwell on the Kent border, near Goudhurst.

For this attack on a member of his entourage Henry exacted swift retribution. He took hostages and had them slaughtered. The *Chronicle of Battel Abbey* describes what happened vividly: 'When the king heard of this he caused many of the people of the country who were assembled above Flimwell whither they had been ordered by Lord John de la Haye, an adherent of the barons, to be surrounded like so many innocent lambs in the fold, and beheaded.'

A total of 315 archers had their heads chopped off in the presence of the king in the parish of St Mary at Ticehurst on that May day. The royal party then moved on to the abbey at Robertsbridge where the king was hospitably entertained by the Cistercian monks.

But he did not have such a good reception from the Benedictines at Battle on May 3. They came out to meet him in solemn procession and the king was not pleased. 'Putting on a wrathful countenance' he demanded from the abbot 100 marks and his son, Edward, asked for an additional forty marks, as compensation for the ambush at Flimwell, in which they believed some of the abbot's men had taken part.

The Cinque Port and Ancient Town of Winchelsea had the doubtful pleasure of entertaining the king and his entire army from May 4 to 8. It had been a tough and dry journey through the forest tracks of the Weald so the soldiers fell eagerly upon Winchelsea's large stocks of wine and soon were exceedingly drunk. As a result 'the whole country was exposed to depredation and rapine.'

Henry, having as he thought secured the support of the citizens of Winchelsea and the use of their ships, should he need them, returned to the Benedictines at Battle. He arrived there to learn that de Montfort and the barons were on their way to meet him. Scouts were sent out to see who was where and, directing his course by their intelligence, Henry ordered his army to march towards Lewes.

When the king stopped for the night at Herstmonceux another of his company was killed, but this time it was an accident and retribution was not exacted. A chance blow in the throat from an arrow caused the death of Roger de Tournay while the troops were 'hunting and destroying the park.'

On May 11 Henry and his army arrived at Lewes and joined forces with the Earl de Warenne. The king went to the Priory of St Pancras while his son, Edward, and his followers chose to stay with the de Warennes as Lewes Castle.

The opposing armies did not clash at once. The Bishop of Chichester tried to make peace between the king and de Montfort, who had set up camp at his manor of Fletching, some eight miles to the north. There was much to-ing and fro-ing by emissaries from either side but on May 13 negotiations broke down. It was war.

The king and his army commanders were still asleep - after a night of carousing, according to Franciscan monk, Richard of Durham - when at dawn the next day a patrol spotted de Montfort's troops advancing on the Downs above Lewes. They had prepared for the battle by prayer and confessing their sins and they were wearing white crosses to demonstrate the virtue of their cause.

After a hasty council of war to decide the line of battle Henry's army followed his banner of the red dragon to confront the enemy. The impetuosity of Prince Edward probably lost the day for the

Hand to hand fighting in the streets of Lewes and a hand held cannon firing from the castle battlements. That is how this illustrator of Holinshed's *Chronicles* depicted he conflict some 300 years after it took place..

royalists as, after putting a division of Londoners to flight, he pursued the retreating soldiers for far longer than necessary, leaving his father's troops to face a strong counter-attack from de Montfort's other forces.

Henry fought bravely. He was 'much beaten about by swords and maces and had two horses killed under him,' but between sunrise and noon most of his army was destroyed. He managed to get back to his headquartyers at the Priory of St Pancras and Edward, on his return to Lewes, fought his way through de Montfort's troops to his father's side.

De Montfort, having cornered the king, set a lot of the town on fire with burning arrows to smoke out any royalist supporters who might be in hiding. He even set the priory church alight but the blaze was soon extinguished.

After the battle came the negotiations, with the monks acting as go-between, as one side made proposals and the other produced counter-proposals. Eventually a settlement was reached an on May 16, 1246 the Mise of Lewes was signed and the seeds of constitutional government were sown.

Henry spent the night of May 17 at Battle Abbey on his way to London and the monks expressed themselves delighted to have 'the wrongdoer, humiliated and harmless, again at their door.' He was the last king to fight a battle on Sussex soil. It was one which caused the death of some 8,000 people and the bones of 1,500 victims of the conflict were discovered in 1810, buried in three pits on land where Lewes prison now stands.

The 700th anniversary of the Battle of Lewes was marked by this monument in the Priory grounds. It is the work of Italian sculptor Enzo Palazotta and the bronze frieze round the helmet depicts scenes from the conflict.

# 3

# KINGS IN THE COUNTY

## Edward I - III

EDWARD I, who succeeded his father in 1272, happily proved, as far as Sussex was concerned, more of a developer than a dealer of death. As Prince of Wales he had been escorted, spurless and a prisoner, to Dover after the Battle of Lewes, but two years later he was issuing instructions about the conduct of the citizens of the Cinque Port of Winchelsea, a town he visited frequently and in which he was interested.

He was a keen advocate of the rule of law and disliked undisciplined behaviour wherever he encountered it. He required the

King Edward I

people of Winchelsea to give up piracy, a pastime in which they indulged whenever the fishing was poor. For 'acts of savage barbarity at sea a lot of guilty blood was spilled - although the multitude was spared,' says the *Chronicle of Battel Abbey*.

The harbour at Winchelsea was still intact and in constant use, but the town itself was becoming more and more derelict as the inhabitants moved inland to avoid the encroaching sea. Those who remained had difficulty in making a living which perhaps explains Edward's order to the barons and bailiffs of the Cinque Ports in 1272 to expel all the Jews from the town without delay 'as it is not a town they are accustomed to inhabit.' Almost to a man the Jews were the moneylenders of medieval England and they had a habit of moving to communities in financial distress where they knew their business would be brisk.

The king came south himself to see what could be done about the sea-stressed town. He decided that it would have to be rebuilt further inland and chose a site on high ground in the neighouring manor of Iham. But before he could settle down at the drawing board and plan the new town he had important business at the other end of the county.

With his queen, Eleanor of Castile, and all the court, he was at Chichester cathedral on June 16, 1276 for a ceremony to mark the removal of the bones of St Richard from their original burial place in the nave to a new shrine behind the altar screen.

The king and queen stayed for three days at the Bishop's Palace at Aldingbourne, four miles to the east, while the Chichester celebrations were going on, and Edward paid a harpist called Lovel 6s. 6d. for singing the praises of St Richard at the cathedral.

A fortnight later he was at Lewes, the scene of the narrow defeat of his father's forces. He stayed at the Priory of St Pancras for six days, issuing various orders to the Cinque Ports and no doubt recalling with old comrades the triumphs and the tragedies of the battle. Edward then made his way via Laughton and Battle, to have another look at Winchelsea.

The town with its 300 houses and fifty inns was disappearing fast beneath the waves so something had to be done - and quickly. Edward produced his plans and ordered the warden of the Cinque Ports, Stephen de Penchester, and other officers to start the building work at Iham at once. His design was for blocks of houses divided by a parallel series of streets intersecting each other at right angles. There was to be a market place, two churches, dedicated to St Thomas and St Giles as at old Winchelsea, and a monastery for the Grey Friars and gates on all the approach roads. One of the original gates, the Strand Gate, still stands.

However busy he was with administering his kingdom, leading his troops on Crusades and campaigns, and founding new towns - he was also responsible for Kingston upon Hull - King Edward never forgot his religious observances. He had a particular attachment to St Richard of Chichester. He visited the saint's new shrine a number of times and he and his family presented many gifts to it including clasps of gold, gilt cups, and gold embroidered robes. The cost and weights of the individual items are carefully itemised in the royal wardrobe accounts.

He was also generous to living clerics as well as dead ones. When staying at Arundel on one of his progresses through the county he gave the preaching friars there twenty two shillings for three days food. On another occasion they received thirteen shillings for three days food and 6s. 5d. was spent on grass for the royal horses and ten shillings for poultry for the castle kitchen. His daily expenditure when on tour, bringing government to the people before improved communications and the establishment of some form of local government made this unnecessary, averaged £38 8s. 5d. Out of this amount four shillings went regularly on alms to the poor.

The rich were expected to give rather than to receive and the royal entourage relied for much of its sustenance on the generosity of the nobility and the religious houses in the areas it visited. On one of his summer visits to Arundel Edward received six carcases of oxen, three and a half sheep, seven and three quarter pigs and one and a quarter sides of bacon for his household. At Lewes he was given two oxen, three pigs and six sheep by the prior and received the same amount of meat at Chichester three days later from Master John de Laci. The sheriff of Sussex produced four oxen, four pigs and six sheep and the citizens of Chichester two oxen and a cask of wine.

For the defence of his realm Edward was building up the navy and he found Sir William de Echyngham's fortified manor of Udimore a convenient base from which to visit the harbours of the Cinque Ports.  It was from there, on November 2, 1294, he prorogued Parliament giving, as his reason for doing so, the need for him to stay in the Winchelsea area 'in order to congregate and prepare our fleet, which we hope, by the favour of God, will be most profitable for the defence of the kingdom.'

The king was back at Udimore eighteen months later. In the

interval he had been up north conquering the Scots and could now turn his attention to the French. When he was at Udimore he visited Brede and was furious to find that the Abbot of Fecamp had built a prison there. 'It is not a prison but a house of detention for the safe custody of thieves,' argued the abbot who held the manor of Brede through a charter from Edward the Confessor. But Edward would have none of it and swiftly convened a court at Brede and released from the prison John Comyn and John Meredith 'to serve him against the King of France and other enemies.'

By August 1297 Edward was ready to set sail for France. He was at Winchelsea for a final review of the fleet when he had a narrow escape from serious injury. The horse he was riding was frightened by the noise made by the sails of a windmill and refused to pass it. He urged the animal on with spurs and whip and it leapt over a wall onto the road below, landing safely but slipping deep into the mud. The king managed to stay in the saddle and turn the horse round and ride back through the land gate. The people who were waiting for him were 'filled with wonder and delight at his miraculous escape,' says Thomas of Walsingham in his account of the incident.

On August 22, 1297 Edward, aboard a vessel bearing his name, led his fleet of 350 ships from Winchelsea outward bound for Flanders. He did not return to Sussex until the summer of 1299. He was with his court at Lamberhurst on June 21 and gave seven shillings to the chapel there as a thank offering for the good news he had received from France - the signing of the Treaty of Montreuil and the arrangement of his marriage to Margaret, sister of the King of France. The following day he was at Mayfield where he stayed at the Archbishop's Palace and offered seven shillings at the chapel in honour of St Alban, whose feast day it was.

The night of June 23 he spent as the guest of Arnald at Uckfield. And what a night that was. Perhaps euphoria about the king's betrothal to a beautiful woman, a worthy successor to Queen Eleanor who had died in 1291, had put everyone in a party mood for eighty two gallons of beer were consumed and a certain

This view of the Strand Gate, Winchelsea, from a 19th century engraving, gives some idea of the steepness of the bank down which the king's horse fell.

amount of damage was done, some of it by the royal bridegroom-to-be. The stewards' accounts for the next day have this entry: 'To Arnald de Uckfield, host to the king, to damage done to his house and curtilage by the arrival of the king at the same place. By gift of the same king in compensation to him for damage done by His Majesty's own hands at the same place and day - 20s.'

The court was at Lewes on June 24 and 25 and the usual gift of three days food was given to the Franciscans at the friary near Cliffe Bridge. The king also punished a number of local tradesmen for giving short weight. Among those to feel the royal wrath were some innkeepers from Southover and the Cliffe who were each fined 6s. 8d. for 'transgression of their measures' and some bakers from Seaford for 'deficiency found in their loaves.'

His son, Prince Edward, then a fifteen  year old, was with him at Lewes. Apparently the boy had a liking for plain, wholesome food for the clerk of the pantry received 6s. 8d. for 'the carriage of the bread and butter of the king's son.' When the royal household moved on to Bramber the prince stayed in Lewes where he had discovered a large kennel of hounds. His interest in the animals was encouraged by his fond father, who paid eight shillings to Thomas de Erlham to bring some dogs from Bramber to Lewes to add to the pack.

At Chichester on June 28 the king made his usual pilgrimage to the shrine of St Richard before moving on to Petworth and then to Horsham where a number of local tradesmen were brought before him accused of giving short measures of bread and beer.

Before his marriage to Margaret in Canterbury cathedral on September 10, Edward made another brief visit to the shrine of St Richard and his steward took the opportunity to buy 100 gallons of beer from Marieta de Kythenere for 8s. 4d., seven sheep from Henry le Botiller for 10s. 4d., and an ox from Stephen Ode for nine shillings, perhaps in preparation for the wedding feast.

The royal household made another progress from Surrey through Sussex to Kent in September 1302, staying at religious houses at East Dean, Chichester, and Slindon; at Arundel and Bramber castles; at the Priory of St Pancras in Lewes, with the Augustinians at Michelham Priory; at Herstmonceux Castle and at Battle Abbey. At Slindon, where the Archbishop of Canterbury had a palace on the foundations of which Slindon House now stands, swans and peacocks were supplied for the royal table as well as the usual oxen, sheep, pigs and poultry. These swans were the property of the archbishop and reared for him at Pagham harbour.

King Edward I's last visit to the county was in 1305. By then he was sixty six and in failing health and his condition was not helped by the bad behaviour of his son who he had to punish with three months' banishment when the court was at Midhurst on June 13. He then moved to Cocking, where the Earls of Arundel had a house, and a few days later he went to Chichester to visit the shrine of St Richard.

On this occasion 300lbs of wax costing £15 1s. 0d, was bought to make a candle of the same height as the king, who was not called Longshanks for nothing - he was a very tall man. Its wick was consecrated by touching it to the relics of St Richard and then it was burnt before the shrine in the hope that it would help the king recover his health.

Perhaps Edward felt better after the candle was consumed for on June 19 he went to Arundel and from the castle there rode over to Findon. He was back at Arundel on June 20 and then went to Shoreham with the queen where he paid Thomas de Weston the sum of £1   2s. 0d. for grass for her horses before moving to Clayton where the court spent the night of June 22. Next stop was Lewes for a three day stay at the Priory of St Pancras. Here the queen's horses were re-shod at a cost of 3s.   5d  and the king went over the Downs on different days to West Dean, Horsted and Buxted to deal with various minor legal matters, before journeying on to Mayfield and then to Bayham Abbey, where he spent his last night in Sussex on June 2.

A year later, on his way to ravage Scotland with fire and sword, the king died.  With his last breath he commanded his son not to bury him, nor to be crowned, until Scotland was subdued. But the young man disregarded his father's dying wishes and sent the late king's body to Westminster for burial, abandoned the Scottish war and made lavish plans for his own coronation.

The romantic ruins of Bayham Abbey, where so many Plantagenet kings enjoyed the hospitality of the Premonstratensians.

PRINCE EDWARD, when he was at Lewes in 1299, had taken a great interest in a kennel of hounds he found there and may well have bought the animals or perhaps hunted with them. Certainly he had a stud of horses at Ditchling from 1304 - another present from his devoted dad.

Although the young prince was not popular with the nobility and given, according to William de Knighton, to 'the company of singers, actors, grooms, labourers, rowers, sailors and other mechanics', he took his horse and dog breeding seriously.

Among a bundle of his letters discovered in the chapter house at Westminster are a number referring to the Ditchling stud which his father bought for him from the executors of John de Warenne, Lord of Lewes. The prince played an active part in the negotiations. In one letter he stipulates that there must be an independent assessment of the value of the stud and the horses must not be moved until they have been examined. In another letter he asks the executors how much is owed in wages to 'John de Dychenynge, Keeper of the King's Colts, while in the late earl's service' and will they kindly settle this account; and in a third he asks his friend Robert de Winchelsea, Archbishop of Canterbury, for the loan of a good stallion for the improvement of the stud. He gives an undertaking that if a stallion is sent to Ditchling it will be well cared for and returned in good condition at the end of the season.

Nothing remains today to indicate where in Ditchling the king's colts were kept. The stud may have been in the Lodge Hill/Broad Hill area, once part of a Saxon royal manor which was divided up by the de Warennes and either sold or given to the monks of Lewes Priory.

Prince Edward was enjoying his visits to Sussex well enough until June 13, 1305. On that day he joined his father's court at Midhurst only to find that the news of his deer poaching activities with his friend, Piers Gaveston, had been reported to the king by a furious Bishop of Chester.

In a letter to an old family friend, Henry de Lacy, Earl of Lincoln, Edward describes the royal wrath: 'He is so angry with us that he has forbidden us that neither ourselves nor any of our suite should be so bold as to enter within his household,' he writes. 'And he has forbidden all officers of his household and of the Exchequer that they should neither give us or lend us anything whatever for the sustenance of our household.'

The prince, suddenly penniless, stayed on at Midhurst for a few days hoping for his father's forgiveness. When this was not forthcoming he decided to follow the royal progress through Sussex at a safe distance 'until we may be able to recover his good pleasure for which we have a great desire.'

As he could not pay his followers he had to dismiss them, and he tried hard to find them other jobs. He wrote a series of begging letters to bishops in an attempt to get them church appointments, and made repeated, but unsuccessful, efforts to persuade the Bishop of Chichester to give the next prebendary vacancy at the cathedral to the keeper of his wardrobe, Sir Walter Reynaud.

The first of these letters was written on June 18 at Singleton where the prince was staying at the Earl of Arundel's hunting lodge at Downley. On June 20 he was at the Bishop of Chichester's palace at Aldingbourne and wrote from there to Sir Walter Reynaud asking for suitable clothes and riding horses for his attendance on Queen Mary, Dowager Queen of France and her son, who were planning a State visit.

'It will be our duty to meet them and accompany them as long as they shall be in these parts and therefore it will become us to be well mounted with palfreys and well apparelled with robes and other things against their coming,' he wrote. 'We command that you cause to be brought for our use two palfreys handsome and suitable for riding and two saddles with the best reins that we have and the best and finest cloth that you can find for sale in London for two or three robes for our use with fur, and satin, and all things proper for them.'

On June 23 the prince was staying near Edburton and the next day he wrote from Rodmell, near Lewes, to his treasurer asking about his rents in Wales, and to his younger brothers, Thomas and Edmund, inquiring after their health. On June 25 and 26 he was at Lewes, on June 27 at Hellingly and on June 28 and 29 with the Benedictines at Battle Abbey.

On July 5 he caught up with the king at Canterbury and found his father in a forgiving mood and prepared to give him some help with the expenses of his household. The king's wardrobe accounts record the extent of this help and give some idea of the foods favoured by the prince and his followers.

There was a cash advance of 13s. 4d., 1,727lbs of wax, 'for the expenses of the household of the Lord Prince of Wales;' 107lbs of almonds, 'to the same;' 200lbs of rice; 701lbs of sugar; three boxes of gingerbread; 440lbs of ginger; 21lbs of cinnamon; 44lbs of peppercorns; 2lbs of nutmeg; 1lb of mace; 7lbs of saffron; 26lbs of fennel seed; 14lbs of cummin; fifteen baskets of figs; six baskets of raisins; and one bale or 252lbs of dates. It would appear that the prince liked a good curry, had a sweet tooth, and no longer demanded bread and butter.

Edward II visited Sussex only once as king. In the summer of 1324 he called on the Premonstratensians at Bayham Abbey, the Cistercians at Robertsbridge and the hospitable Benedictines at Battle where, on August 28, he offered at the great altar seven shillings and a cloth of gold and red silk worth fifty shillings. The following day he gave a silver gilt cup, carved with baboons and valued at eight shillings, from the store at the Tower of London, to the master of the sailing ship La Juliano which had bought him a cargo of luxury goods from Spain. Shipbuilder John Pain from Winchelsea was also a target for the royal generosity, receiving a gift of four shillings when he arrived at the abbey to tell the king that the ship he had ordered, La Nicolas de Winchelsea, had been completed.

Local landowners showered the king and his court with good things to eat and drink. These gifts, and their givers, were faithfully recorded in the wardrobe accounts and included: 'From Robert Acheland, four rabbits, six swans, three herons; from Stephen Acheland three rabbits, ten flagons of wine and two flagons of sweet wine; from Edmund Passelewe three carcases of oxen and twelve carcases of mutton; and from William de Echynham two oxen, six sheep, three peacocks. three pike and twelve bream.' The abbot of Battle, Alan de Ketling, chipped in with eighty four loaves of bread, a cask of wine, two oxen, three pigs, six carcases of mutton, two swans, two rabbits, three herons, three pheasants, a dozen capons, two pike and twelve bream.

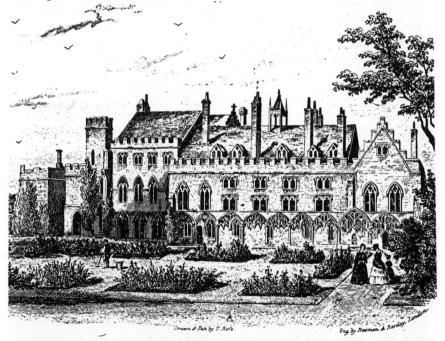

The remains of the cloister of Battle Abbey, where medieval monarchs and Benedictine monks once used to walk, can be seen in the foreground of this 19th century engraving.

The court moved to Pevensey on August 30 and there, perhaps while eating one of the 500 pears and 1,000 large nuts sent down from London for him, the king signed documents appointing Edmund de Passelewe warden of the port of Rye and William de Echyngham warden of the port of Winchelsea. These appointments may or may not have been influenced by the lavishness of their gifts to him at Battle, but the official reason was fear of invasion of the large harbour of Winchelsea by the French while the Cinque Ports' ships were with the fleet at Portsmouth.

The little village of Bourne, now Eastbourne, had to provide food and drink for the court on September 1 and bravely coped with the burden of hospitality, producing cheese, wine, wax, oats, three quarters of beef, three carcases of mutton, one and a half hogs, five rabbits and one bream. The expenses of the royal household are listed as 30s. 4d. for the kitchen; 59s. 6d. for wages; four shillings for alms; 17s. 4d. for the dispensary; 7s. 10d. for butlery; 5s. 3d. for wardrobe and 71s. 9d. for stabling.

There is no record of the king visiting the Ditchling stud when he spent the weekend of August 31 to September 2 at the Bishop of Chichester's manor of Bishopstone but he could well have done so. On September 3 he was with the Knights Templar at Shipley, incurring household expenses of 10s. 3d. This seems the average for a night's stay as similar sums are recorded in respect of Horsham and Newbridge where, on September 5, the king gave a silver gilt and enamelled cup worth fifty shillings to the messenger who brought him news of the Earl of Richmond's release from imprisonment by the Scots.

There were more fruit and nuts on the royal table at Petworth. The rector provided 140 pears and William de Zouche produced ninety six filberts and twenty eight flagons of wine, two flagons of beer, two oxen, four swans and six herons. Music was provided by Nicolas the harpist who received twenty shillings from the king's own hand.

Edward II left Sussex on September 8, 1324, his packhorses laden with gifts and his heart no doubt warmed by the welcome he had received. Three years later he was deposed by his peers. They had become increasingly enraged at his profligate behaviour towards his new favourite, Hugh de Despenser, to whom he had given, among other things, the port of Shoreham. On January 13, 1327 they exercised their constitutional rights and replaced him with his son - Edward III.

As the new king was only fourteen the country was ruled for four years by a regency of nobles with the real power in the hands of his widowed mother, Isabella of France, and her favourite, Roger Mortimer.

EDWARD III had been married to Philippa of Hainault for three years and had a son - the Black Prince - when he claimed his kingdom at the age of eighteen and had Isabella made a prisoner of state and Mortimer hanged without trial at Tyburn.

It was through his disgraced mother that Edward had a claim to the throne of France - a claim the pursuit of which by successive English kings resulted in the Hundred Years' War. But it was a sea battle with Spanish marauders rather than with the French which first brought him to Sussex.

In the spring of 1350 a large Spanish fleet was in the Channel and disrupting trade and troop links between England and Brittany and Gascony. As soon as he got to hear about it the king appointed William Passelewe and Robert Shipman to pick 100 of the best sailors from Kent and Sussex to man his flagship, the 250 ton Thomas, in which he had so decisively defeated the French off Sluys in Flanders ten years earlier. He then settled down to make thorough preparations for the forthcoming conflict.

He had special images made of tin for the masthead streamers of the ships in the fleet and he commissioned an image of St Thomas, at a cost of eight shillings, for his own ship as well as four standards displaying the royal leopards and fleur de lys. He had every intention of being comfortable while at sea for he gave instructions for a feather-bed costing twenty shillings to be put in his cabin, together with four nightcaps and four pillowcases of fine linen, three blankets costing 12s. 2d., two mattresses of different colours costing 15s. 9d., and four folding stools at a shilling each. The court tailor, John Marreys, was ordered to repair with plated brass two swords, their scabbards and belts, and provide 'a haubergeon and other articles of dress for the journey of the king to Winchelsea.'

All this took time, and it was not until August 26 that the king, accompanied by the Black Prince, joined the fleet. The next day they both rode to the de Echyngham's manor house at Udimore where Queen Philippa was staying with her ladies in the hope of getting a grandstand view of the battle. They returned to Winchelsea in the evening to be entertained in the Court Hall by Stephen Alard, leader of the Cinque Ports squadron.

On August 29 the Spaniards, on their way home before the

A Cinque Ports ship of the 13th century, before the steering oar gave way to a fixed rudder. It is drawn from the design on the seal of Winchelsea.

autumn gales, were sighted in the Channel and the English fleet
sailed out to intercept them. The king had boarded the Thomas
the previous day wearing a black velvet jacket and with a small
beaver hat on his head. The court musicians, who had been
provided with silk banners for their trumpets, were commanded
to play a new German dance recently introduced by Battle of
Sluys veteran, Sir John Chandos, who sang to its accompaniment.

The Pelhams, De La Warrs, Burrells, Cowdrays, Wakehursts
and Poynings were among the lords of Sussex who did battle with
their king on that hot summer day. The Spaniards were engaged
in the early evening of August 29 in the melee that was naval
warfare in those days. The ships on both sides were much too
cumbersome and too heavily laden to execute any skilful
manouevres. They relied on getting close enough to use the fire
power of their archers and then to ram and grapple each other to
allow for hand to hand fighting. The Spaniards had the advantage
of larger vessels from which they could rain down a bombardment
of rocks and stones as the English tried to board them, but by
nightfall about half their forty four ships had been captured.

Next morning there was no sign of the remaining Spaniards and
the king sailed back to Winchelsea in triumph. Contemporary
accounts of the conflict vary greatly as to the number of casualties
but all agree that it was a savage battle with heavy damage to
ships of both sides.

The king and the prince rode over to join the queen at Udimore
the moment they stepped ashore and the chronicler, Froissart,
records that 'the night passed in revelry with the ladies. . .' The
next day a thanksgiving service was held at St Thomas Church,
Winchelsea, and Edward stayed at Udimore until September 3,
holding regular courts at which pardons were issued for earlier
transgressions to men in the retinues of the Black Prince and
some of the noble lords.

Another triumph, this time a diplomatic one, brought the king
back to Sussex ten years later. He had just negotiated the Peace
of Bretigny by which he gained absolute sovereignty over the
duchy of Aquitaine and retained possession of Calais in exchange
for renouncing his claim to the French throne.

He and the Black Prince landed at Rye on May 18 and rode directly to London, a distance of about sixty miles, arriving there at 9am the next day.

Two years later he was at Winchelsea again and from there adjourned Parliament until November 3. This was the last occasion on which a Plantagenet set foot on Sussex soil and for the county it was the end of years of battles and sea skirmishes, royal feuds and family quarrels and all the rough stuff of British history in the making.

# 4

# PRISONERS AT PEVENSEY

## James and Queen Joan

The Wars of the Roses kept the York and Lancaster kings firmly occupied in the north and west of England in the early part of the fifteenth century. Sussex saw little of them although it played host to two royal prisoners.

In 1406 James, the thirteen year old heir to the throne of Scotland, was captured on his way to France and committed to the care of Sir John Pelham at Pevensey Castle and later at Windsor. Sir John, made Constable of Pevensey and a Knight of the Bath by Henry IV, was given £700 a year to look after young James and he made such a good job of it that his prisoner turned out to be one of the wisest and most accomplished of the kings of Scotland.

Queen Joan of Navarre, the widow of Henry IV, was also committed to the custody of Sir John Pelham at Pevensey. In September 1419 she was arrested by order of her stepson, Henry V, victor of Agincourt, and stripped of her dowry lands, money, furniture and personal possessions. Even the clothes she wore were taken from her. Her offence was, according to the Parliamentary Rolls, that she had 'compassed and imagined the death and destruction of our said lord the king in the most high and horrible manner that could be devised.' Arrested with her were two 'domestic sorcerers,' Roger Colles and Petronal Brocart, who were suspected of the same treason.

Joan's fall from grace was sudden. In the first years of her widowhood she had received nothing but kindness and respect from the new king who was keen to enlist the help of her son, the Duke of Bretagne, when he invaded France. In July 1418 Henry referred to her as his 'dearest mother' when ordering customs officers at the ports of London, Plymouth and Dartmouth not to collect import tax on goods consigned to her from abroad. The duty frees she received on that occasion included three sealed cases of cash, sixty pipes of wine, two bales of the finest linen and a barrel of anchovies.

Sir John dealt as considerately as he could with his prisoner. He was given an advance of £166   13s. 4d. for her maintenance and he immediately provided her with nine servants and her own personal physician. But incarceration without trial cannot have been pleasant for Queen Joan, who was then about forty nine years old.

She had been arrested on the information of her personal confessor, a Minorite friar called John Randolf, but he did not live to testify against her. He was strangled by a fellow cleric with whom he was having a particularly heated argument, so he never did reveal the 'high and horrible' means by which he claimed the widowed queen planned to do away with her stepson.

In the fourth year of her imprisonment she was joined at Pevensey by Sir John Mortimer of the rival House of York. He had made so many attempts to escape from the Tower of London that he was moved to a more secure fortress. But they were not together for long. Henry, by then master of the whole of the north of France, fell ill with dysentry. On July 13, 1422, a month before his death at the age of thirty three, he ordered his council of state to restore the dowager queen's dowry 'which charge we be advised no longer to bear on our conscience.'

The remorseful and conscience-stricken king not only returned Joan's lands, the revenues from which he had used to finance his campaigns in France, but also 'her beds and all other things moveable we had of her.' He also offered her material for five or six gowns, and horses and eleven carts to carry herself and her household to wherever she wanted to go.

Whether Joan got her new gowns and wore them is debatable for she was soon in court mourning for her stepson in a gown made of seven and a half yards of black cloth at seven shillings a yard with a grey squirrel fur collar and cloak for which she paid 23s. 4d. Her household accounts show that she was not a generous employer for payments to individual retainers never exceed  6s. 8d - although she was happy enough to lay down a stock of claret for which she  paid £56  0s. 4d.

HENRY VI, who succeeded his father when only eight months old, visited Sussex twice during his thirty nine year reign and neither occasion is well documented. He was at Chichester in 1447 and again in 1451, possibly for the purpose of appointing justices of the peace. Certainly that is the reason given for Edward IV's two visits to the cathedral city, the first of which was in May 1472 when he was thirty.

On that occasion an order was made for the Exchequer to pay the sum of 6s. 8d for three and a half yards of cloth of gold to make 'a jacquette for the king's person.' The total cost of the materials for this jacket amounted to fifteen shillings and it cost five shillings to hire a horse to transport it, and some chain mail, from London to Chichester.

The king was at Chichester again in September 1479, staying on the way there at the Trotton home of Sir Thomas Leuknor.

# 5

# TUDORS ON TOUR

## Pageantry and picnics

THE Wars of the Roses ended in 1486 with the marriage of Henry VII and Elizabeth of York, which united the warring factions and brought a Tudor to the throne. Henry VII was too busy putting down the rich barons, coping with pretenders to the throne such as Lambert Simnel and Perkin Warbeck, and trying to make as much money as possible to have time to travel round his kingdom except on essential business and usually at the head of an army.

When he died in 1509, leaving a personal fortune of £800,000, and was succeeded by his eighteen year old son, the country was more peaceful - and a lot poorer.

SOCIAL rather than state affairs brought Henry VIII to Sussex. In August 1526, a year before he started trying to get his marriage to Katharine of Aragon annulled, he was invited to Petworth by Henry Algernon Percy, 5th Earl of Northumberland - a nobleman of great wealth and taste. It appears that he enjoyed himself for in his *Letters and Papers* it is recorded that he 'made merry and showed himself very friendly to the local gentry.'

From Petworth he came with his household to Arundel, his host being Thomas Howard, Duke of Norfolk, whose niece, Katharine Howard, was to become his fifth wife. Arundel Castle was much to the king's liking 'though it was then in great decay, differing greatly from Petworth, which was one of the best appointed houses in the land, than which few were more neatly kept or had fairer and pleasanter walks.' The royal tourist then spent a few days at Lord De La Warr's house at Halnaker but any comments he might have made about it are not on record.

Henry made a second visit to Sussex in 1538, staying at Petworth and Arundel and also at Cowdray. These were again private visits to old friends - Cowdray had just been bought by Sir William Fitzwilliam, Lord Keeper of the Privy Seal, Lord High Admiral, and soon to be created the first Earl of Southampton. They were not royal progresses involving the whole court such as the one undertaken by young Edward VI five years after his father's death.

IN the spring of 1552 fourteen year old Edward had measles, followed by smallpox, but by the beginning of May he had recovered sufficiently to consider a progress through the southern counties of his kingdom.

Special liveries were ordered for the sixteen state trumpeters who were to accompany him and the huge sum of £315 4s. spent on red cloth for new liveries for the yeomen, grooms, pages and other attendants of the privy chamber. On June 5 Edmund Standon, clerk of the stable, received £151 from the Exchequer 'towards the furnishing of things necessary for the King's Majesty against this progress.'

On July 21 Edward VI entered Sussex from Surrey with more followers than the county could support. In his *Journal* he wrote: 'The number of bands that were with me on this progress made the train so great it was thought good they should be sent home, save only 150, which were picked out of all the bands. This was because the train was thought to be near 4,000 horse which were enough to eat up the county; for there was little meadow nor hay all the way as I went.'

Edward kept his personal guard and had with him a number of heralds to supervise the ceremonial of the court on its travels.

They were led by Garter King of Arms who received an allowance of ten shillings a day for food between July 5 and October 7, when the court was back at Windsor. Clarenceux and Norroy each had a daily allowance of 6s. 8d; Somerset Herald received four shillings and pursuivants Rouge Dragon and Bluemantle two shillings. The heralds also received twenty shillings from each of the large towns the king entered on his progress but Sussex was spared this expense as, although he stayed at nearby Cowdray and Halnaker, he did not go to the City of Chichester.

The king spent his first four nights in the county at Petworth which was then vested in the crown as its owner, Henry Percy, 6th Earl of Northumberland, had died without an heir in 1537. With him were most of the Privy Council - the Lord Great Chamberlain, the Lord Treasurer, Lord High Admiral, Lord Privy Seal and Mr Secretary Cecil - for the business of government had to be dealt with on a regular basis, even when the court was in transit. Two Privy Council meetings, at which the king presided, were held at Petworth and three at Cowdray and three more at Halnaker.

But it was not all work for young Edward. In a letter to his boyhood friend, Barnaby Fitzpatrick, then campaigning with the

Young Edward VI, recovered from measles and smallpox, made a lengthy and costly progress through the county of Sussex in 1552.

King of France, he wrote: 'While you have been occupied in killing of your enemies, in long marchings, in pained journeys, in extreme heat, in sore skirmishings and divers assaults, we have been occupied in killing of wild beasts, in pleasant journeys, in good fare, in viewing fair countries. . .'

From Petworth the king moved to Cowdray, where he was entertained most lavishly by Sir Anthony Browne. Perhaps too lavishly for he wrote to Barnaby: 'We were marvellously, yea rather excessively, banqueted.' Halnaker, where he stayed until August 4, he described as a 'pretty house beside Chichester.' It had been built by Thomas, 8th Lord De La Warr, when Henry VIII was still married to the first of his six wives, and in its great hall were carved the royal arms of England and Aragon.

A tradition persists in Pevensey that Edward, at the age of ten and after just four months on the throne, stayed there with his attendant physician, Dr Andrew Borde. To this day visitors to the Old Mint House, now an antiques centre, can visit the 'King's Room' on the first floor with its bay windows, timbered ceiling and walls decorated with frescoes.

Edward, a prolific letter writer, makes no mention of this visit and neither does Dr Borde, who at the time was a tenant of the hospital master's house at St Giles in the Fields, London.

If Edward did stay with the droll doctor, who had a brother who held the livings of Pevensey, Westham and Northeye, it is surprising that he does not mention doing so in his letters to his friend Barnaby. For Andrew Borde was a larger than life character with a pleasant sense of humour. He gave up the religious life, after twenty years as a Carthusian monk, saying that he was not able to abide by the 'rigorosity' of the order, and went abroad to study medicine.

On his return to this country in 1530 he cured the Duke of Norfolk of some unspecified malady and was recommended by the grateful peer to King Henry as a physician in waiting. But he did not stay long at court, where his portrait was painted by Holbein. Soon he was on his travels again gathering material for a number of books including his *Handbook of Europe, Breviary of Health, First Book of the Introduction of Knowledge* and his *Itinerary of*

*England.* Also attributed to him are *The Merry Tales of the Wise Men of Gotham* and some say that he was the original Merry Andrew - a name given during Tudor times to clowns, court jesters and buffoons.

WHEN Queen Elizabeth I made her first visit to the county in 1573, a pattern had been established for royal progresses. They served two purposes. They showed the monarch to the people in all her regal splendour and they provided an opportunity for a good spring clean of whatever royal palace the court had vacated. Tudor standards of sanitation were not high and after a few months of concentrated occupation royal homes would smell anything but sweet.

The progresses were slow and not always comfortable even for the queen who, as she grew older and unable to spend the day in the saddle, was carried along on a litter. As the royal household with its waggon train of clothing, furniture and supplies, rumbled its way at a stately twelve miles a day from Greenwich, which it left on July 14, Lord Burleigh wrote to the Earl of Shrewsbury: 'The queen had a hard beginning of her progress in Kent and in some parts of Sussex where surely were more dangerous rocks and valleys and much worse ground than was in the Peak.'

From her 'own house at Knolle,' where she spent five days, the queen went to Lord Bergavenney's manor of Birlingham for three days and then visited Sir Thomas Gresham, founder of the Royal Exchange, at Mayfield. He lived in Mayfield Palace, one of the official residences of the Archbishops of Canterbury from the days of St Dunstan until the Dissolution of the Monasteries. It had been acquired by Sir John Gresham in 1545 when, on the instructions of Henry VIII, Thomas Cranmer was busy selling off church property.

Some parts of the old palace, including the room in which the queen slept, survive to this day as part of St Leonard's Convent, a Roman Catholic school for girls which now occupies the site. Carved on the panelling of this room is the Gresham crest of a grasshopper and the date 1571, the year in which the queen formally opened the Royal Exchange.

The royal entourage then retraced its steps to Eridge, another of Lord Bergavenny's houses, where the queen received the French Ambassador. By having his sovereign to stay twice in a matter of weeks the noble lord patently felt that he had done enough and did not produce any rich gifts for Gloriana. Lord Burleigh noticed the omission. 'These journeys of our good queen were generally attended with considerable expense to her loving subjects,' he writes. 'It was usual for those she honoured with her presence, besides maintaining her retinue, to make her valuable presents in gold and silver. However, among the list of jewels given to Her Majesty on this progress, I do not find any given by Lord Bergavenny.'

After spending three days with Mr Thomas Guldeford at Hempstead, near Benenden, Queen Elizabeth made her way to Rye, stopping at Northiam on the way to have a picnic. She sat in the shade of an oak tree on the village green near the churchyard and dined on dishes provided by Mr George Bysshopp who lived in a house opposite the oak. This picnic spot was so much to her liking that she lunched there again three days later - and changed her shoes. The pair she took off where begged from her attendants

as souvenirs and are preserved to this day in a glass case at Brickwall, now a boys' preparatory school. They are made of a soft green coloured material and have fairly high heels. The oak under the shade of which she dined, also survives on the village green.

Elizabeth was very taken with Rye, where she knighted her host at Hempstead, Thomas Guldeford, as well as Thomas Shirley, Thomas Walsingham and Alexander Culpepper of Bedgebury from whom she had received a crystal cup and cover garnished with silver and gilt and containing a 'tuft of flowers'. She expressed herself much gratified by testimonies of love and loyalty, duty and reverence received from the people - among which had been a purse containing 100 gold half sovereigns or angels - and she referred to the town as 'Rye Royal'.

Her three day stay cost Rye more than £150. The mayor, Henry Gaymer, lent the council £100 and sixty coats were provided for the local militia which escorted the queen into the town. She stayed, it is said, at the Customs House on the west side of the churchyard, which was then called Grene Hall.

The queen was equally impressed by Winchelsea and in response to a loyal address from the mayor and corporation, jokingly called it 'Little London' and commended the industry of its inhabitants, the elegance of its buildings and the deportment of the people.

A planned visit to Lord Buckhurst's newly-built Priory House in Southover, Lewes, had to be abandoned in the summer of 1577 because of the plague, as had visits to Lord Montague at Battle Abbey, and to Lord Arundel at Arundel Castle.

Arrangements for this progress were well in hand when the plague struck. Lord Montague had built new rooms for the queen at Battle Abbey and the prospective hosts had bought up all available delicacies for the table from traders in the surrounding counties.

Lord Buckhurst was a little late in stocking his larder and wrote anxiously to the Earl of Sussex saying he would have to send to Flanders for food 'which he would speedily do if the time of Her Majesty's coming and tarriance with him were certain'.

Mr Henry Goring, who was expecting the queen at Burton Park, near Petworth, for two nights wrote to his friend, Sir William More, with whom she had stayed in Surrey, for advice on how to entertain her. 'Does she bring her own stuff, beer, and other provisions, or did you provide every part?' he asked.

Six years later Elizabeth again thought about coming to Sussex, this time to stay with Henry, 8th Earl of Northumberland, at Petworth, but he proved a reluctant host. On his behalf Sir William Cornwallis wrote to the Secretary of State, Sir Francis Walsingham, saying that although the earl would be delighted to receive the queen there was too little time for adequate preparations to be made, the countess was in poor health, and the Sussex roads were in dreadful state. Sir Francis got the message and the visit did not take place.

The effigy of that most lavish of hosts, Sir Anthony Browne, in Battle Church.

However there was no reluctance on the part of that most lavish of hosts, Lord Montague, to welcome the queen to Cowdray in August, 1591. As Sir Anthony Browne he had 'excessively banqueted' her half brother, Edward VI, and planned to make Elizabeth I's visit even more memorable.

A full account of the entertainment provided over the six days the court was at Cowdray was printed in the same year and sold by William Wright of St Paul's Churchyard so all the world would know the extent and splendour of Sussex hospitality.

The queen 'with a great train', arrived at 8pm on August 15, having dined at Farnham en route. Loud music played as she crossed the bridge into Cowdray and stopped suddenly as a man dressed in armour appeared. He carried a club in one had, a gold key in the other, and stood between two wooden effigies at the main door.

From this vantage point he informed the queen that, when the first stone of the house was laid, there was a prophecy that the walls would shake and the roof totter 'until the wisest, the fairest and most fortunate of all creatures should arrive.' He then handed the queen the gold key declaring that, as 'the Miracle of Time, Nature's Glory and Fortune's Empress' had arrived, the house in future would be immoveable.

This was just the first of a number of fulsome orations the queen had to listen to from strangely-costumed characters during her stay. She accepted the key graciously, said she could swear to the fidelity of the master of the house, embraced Lady Montague and her daughter, Lady Dormer, and decided to have an early night after her journey.

Sunday was spent quietly by the court, no doubt digesting the thirty oxen and 140 geese consumed at breakfast. An elegant hunt was arranged for the queen on Monday. She rode with her entourage into Cowdray Park where 'a delicate bower had been prepared under which her musicians played.' She was handed a crossbow and shot at thirty deer driven into the paddock, killing three of them.

Lady Kildare, Lord Montague's sister, had the temerity to shoot as well and killed one stag. The queen was furious and banned her from the royal table for daring to demonstrate that she also had skill with the bow. Not until the New Year was she forgiven and permitted to present a gift to her sovereign.

After dinner at Cowdray, which lasted until about 6pm, the queen was taken to a turret room from which she watched greyhounds pull down sixteen bucks.

On Tuesday the court was 'beautifully feasted' in the great hall of Easebourne Priory, now used as a parish room. In the afternoon the queen had to listen to more expressions of love and loyalty as she walked in the gardens. First a 'wildman dressed in ivy' popped out from behind an oak and said nice things about her for a long time, then a 'pilgrim dressed in russet' gave another fulsome address before escorting the queen to a tree from which hung the coats of arms of all the noblemen and gentlemen of Sussex. When she had admired this display of colourful escutcheons the sound of a horn signalled 'a most excellent cry of hounds' and three bucks were killed by the buckhounds before the royal party returned to Cowdray for supper.

Wednesday was the day for fishing. The queen's fondness for al fresco feasting was indulged by a dinner set out in an avenue of oaks on a table twenty four yards long. Delicate music accompanied the meal after which the queen was escorted to a 'goodlie fishpond' where an angler delivered yet another lengthy loyal address. The pond was then netted and all the fish from it laid at Her Majesty's feet.

On Thursday more lords and ladies had joined the royal party and a table forty eight yards long was needed to accommodate them at dinner in the oak avenue. In the evening county dignatories were presented to the queen and there was a 'pleasant dance with tabor and pipe.' Lord and Lady Montague joined in 'to the gentle applause of Her Majesty'.

The royal party left Cowdray on Friday for Chichester escorted by Lord Montague and his sons, the sheriff of the shire and a 'goodly company of gentlemen'. As a gesture of appreciation for the hospitality she had received the queen knighted her host's second son, George Browne, and his son-in-law Robert Dormer, as well as four gentlemen of Sussex - Henry Goring of Burton Park, who was so anxious to know if she brought her own provisions with her; Henry Glanham, John Carryll and Nicholas Parker.

The City of Chichester has now no record of the royal visit of August 22. But certainly one did exist for, in a manuscript index of the Corporation registers, is the entry: '1591 - The manner of the queen's reception and entertainment in the Progress to Chichester and the rewards given by the City to the Queen's Officers'.

From records that have survived we learn that the queen slept in what is now an inn in East Street - the Royal Arms. Then it was Scarborough House, the town residence of John, Lord Lumley, her friend and adviser.

He obviously had a part in the forward planning of the progress for he had time to bring over craftsmen from Italy to make the decorative mouldings that adorn the ceiling of the first floor room in which the queen received the mayor and citizens of Chichester. This room, now part of the private apartments of the licensee of the Royal Arms, has been preserved in all its splendour.

Lord Lumley was again host to the queen as the progress continued into Hampshire. On her way to Portsmouth she stopped for the night at Stanstead, an estate he had recently acquired from his father-in-law, Henry Fitzalan, Earl of Arundel, a twice-widowed suitor for the queen's hand in the early years of her reign. On her arrival the queen is credited with another royal witticism. 'Stand, steed' she is alleged to have said as she reined in her horse at the entrance to the estate.

# 6

# RELICS OF THE STUARTS

## The Royal Escape

RELICS of a king who never came here are preserved in the East Sussex village of Ashburnham, near Battle. They used to be kept in the church where they could be touched by people suffering from scrofula, or the king's evil - a tubercular infection of the lymphatic glands.

From the time of Edward the Confessor it was believed that the touch of the sovereign's hands could cure a sufferer from the complaint and in the days of the Stuarts there was a recognised form of service for the touching ceremony which remained in the prayer book until 1719.

Charles II was the most touching of all the monarchs - laying his hands on a total of 92,107 of his subjects. The last person in England to be touched was Dr Samuel Johnson in 1711. He was

A touchpiece from the time of Elizabeth I. On one side is St George slaying the dragon and on the other, the royal arms on a 16th century ship

Clothing of a king who was executed. These relics of Charles I were on display in Ashburnham Church until 1830 when the box was broken into.

thirty months old when he was brought before Queen Anne, who, in accordance with tradition, gave the child a small gold coin or touchpiece to commemorate the occasion.

But as late as 1859 a child was wrapped in a sheet from among the Ashburnham relics of Charles I in the hope of obtaining a cure. This sheet, which bears the monogram CR and a crown embroidered in red thread, was said to have been thrown over the body of the king after his execution. It was given, together with the king's bloodstained shirt, his silk drawers, his garters and his watch to John Ashburnham, a groom of the bedchamber, who attended Charles at the scaffold.

The relics, to which were added a lock of the king's hair, obtained when the royal coffin was opened in 1815, were bequeathed by one of John's descendants, Bernard Ashburnham, to the parish clerks of Ashburnham in perpetuity. From 1783 to 1830 they were kept in the church, but in that year the box containing them was broken into and the outer case of the watch was stolen. The relics were removed to Ashburnham Place for safe keeping and they are still there, being looked after by the present occupants, the Ashburnham Christian Trust.

The next monarch to visit Sussex was Charles II - and his was a flying visit. After the defeat of his forces at the Battle of

Worcester he became a fugitive, hiding in oak trees and doing his best to make his way south to take ship for France. He took the name of Will Jackson and disguised himself as a Puritan, wearing green breeches, a linen shirt, a leather jacket with pewter buttons and a high crowned black hat. With him was Lord Wilmot, whose friend, Colonel George Gunter, was trying to arrange for a suitable ship for the royal escape.

The colonel got in touch with a Chichester merchant, Francis Mansell, who did a lot of trade with France. He called in Nicholas Tettersall, owner of the Shoreham-based coal brig, Surprise, and asked him to carry a friend of the colonel's, who he said had been involved in an illegal duel, secretly across to Normandy. Tettersall was offered £50 for the charter but stuck out for £60 and the deal was struck.

It was a bright October morning in 1651 when the king rode in from Hampshire accompanied by the colonel, Lord Wilmot and Robert Swan, his manservant. They managed to avoid a party of Parliamentarians in Arundel by cutting to the north of the town and taking the steep hill down to Houghton. There they stopped at the inn, the George and Dragon, for a drink. They did not dismount but were served in the saddle with bread and beer and shared out the ox tongue that Colonel Gunter had thoughtfully collected from the kitchen of his sister's house at Hambledon when he started out.

At Bramber they ran into trouble again. The place was packed with soldiers but they had to cross the River Adur somehow and decided to risk riding boldly past the castle and over the bridge. No one challenged them but, after this second near miss, the colonel volunteered to ride on to Brighton to check if the coast was clear and then send word back to the king who, in the meantime, would find somewhere to hide - and rest.

Gunter found Brighton free of Parliamentary forces and reserved the best rooms at the George in West Street. When he was joined there by the king and Lord Wilmot word was sent to Mansell and Tettersall, and they arrived to finalise arrangements to take the mythical duellist to France.

It did not take the crafty captain long to see through his

prospective passenger's disguise. 'He is the King, and I very well know him to be so,' he announced. 'He took my ship, with other fishing vessels from Brighthelmstone, in the year 1648.'

While protesting his loyalty and willingness to help, Tettersall also mentioned that that there was a £1,000 reward for any information leading to the discovery of the king. He insisted that his ship should be insured for £200, just in case. Colonel Gunter reluctantly agreed, and by now doubtful of Tettersall's loyalty, was even more reluctant to let him go home alone to get a clean shirt and muster his crew.

Before dawn next day the party left the inn by the back door and rode along the beach to Shoreham where the Surprise lay aground. She floated on the tide and Tettersall, after telling his crew they were on a secret mission for which all would be well rewarded, set his usual course westwards, so not to arouse suspicion, before turning towards France.

On passage the king sat quietly on deck, keenly watched by a sailor who was smoking a pipe. When Tattersell rebuked the man for staring at his passenger, he replied, with innocent accuracy: 'Surely a cat may look at a king'.

Nine years later Charles was recalled by the Convention Parliament and England became a monarchy once again. Nicholas Tettersall and others who had helped in the royal escape waited expectantly for some form of reward or recognition but nothing was forthcoming. The king seemed to have forgotten about the Surprise and his voyage aboard her. Tettersall decided to remind him of it and sailed the brig to London and moored her opposite Whitehall. Charles took the hint and the Surprise was taken into the navy as an unarmed smack of the fifth rate, under the name of The Royal Escape. Tettersall received a ring from the royal finger and a pension of £100 a year for himself and his descendants.

The ring passed into the possession of the Shiffner family of Coombe Place, Offham, near Lewes, who were related by marriage to Sir John Bridger, the last of Tettersall's descendants to receive the royal pension. Tettersall was also given a commission and the command of a frigate, but he did not last for long in the navy. He was dismissed the service for acting in an unbecoming fashion in a naval engagement.

Just what he did that was unbecoming is not disclosed, and it did not harm his reputation, for on his return to Brighton he was elected High Constable - an office then carrying a fair amount of civic power. In 1670 he bought a parcel of property on the sea front including the Old Ship Hotel - which today has a bar named after him. He died in 1674 and is buried, with his wife, in St Nicholas churchyard. On his tombstone is a now barely decipherable sixteen line epitaph, supposedly written by his son, who is also buried there. It reads:

> Within this marble Monument doth lie
> Approved faith, honour and loyalty;
> In this cold clay he hath now ta'en up his station,
> Who once preserved the church, the crowne and nation.
> When Charles the Greate was nothing but a breath,
> This valiant soul stept 'tween him and death;
> Usurper's threats, nor tyrant rebels' frowne.
> Could not affright his duty to the crowne;
> Which glorious act of his, for church and state,
> Eight Princes, on one day, did gratulate -
> Professing all to him in debt to bee,
> As all the world are to his memory;
> Since earth could not reward the worth him given,
> He now receives it from the King of Heaven.
> In the same chest one jewel more you have,
> The partner of his virtues, bed and grave.

The fleeing Charles was the first of the Stuarts to visit Sussex. Queen Anne was the last. The closest James II came to any association with the county was when he was appointed Lord Warden of the Cinque Ports by his brother at the Restoration.

WILLIAM of Orange - who was invited with his wife, Mary, the youngest daughter of James II, to accept the throne of England in 1689 - did, however, come here.

In February 1692, on his way to Holland, he was entertained at Stanstead by the Earl of Scarborough who, as Richard, Lord Lumley, had been one of the signatories to the invitation for William to come with an army and save England from popery.

The king brought with him his friend, the Grand Duke of Tuscany, and they had a day's fox hunting with the Charlton Hunt. The fame of the hunt, which numbered among its members and guests the Dukes of Richmond, Devonshire, Bolton, Grafton, Montrose, St Albans, and Kingston, and a host of assorted earls and barons, had spread to the Continent when its manager and master was a Mr Roper. Invitations to join the chase, and afterwards talk over the adventures of the day at Foxhall, the banqueting room built at Charlton by the Earl of Burlington, were much sought after by the nobility of France and Germany .

ANNE, before she came to the throne in 1702, paid a brief visit to Charles Seymour, the sixth Duke of Somerset, at Petworth. Apparently she had just as much trouble as did Elizabeth I with the Sussex roads, and carthorses were needed to drag her carriage through the mud.

# 7

# HANOVERIAN HOLIDAYS

## Georgian Sussex

THE start of Sussex by the Sea with the development of the resort towns of Bognor, Brighton, Eastbourne and Worthing was due almost entirely to the House of Hanover, with, in the case of Brighton, a little help from Dr Richard Russell and his sea water cure for assorted ills. Hanoverian kings and their queens, princes, princesses and many a royal duke came to the coast for their health or for a holiday.

George I visited Sussex once intentionally and once unintentionally. This short, shy, elderly German gentleman spoke hardly any English and did not understand a word of the loyal address presented to him by the mayor of Chichester at Stanstead in August 1722. But he graciously acknowledged each member of the council as they were introduced to him by the 1st Duke of Richmond, a Lord of the Bedchamber. His reception of them made up in some part for the disappointment they felt six years earlier when his son, the Prince of Wales, failed to stop there on his way to Stanstead.

Prince George had arranged to review the fort, docks and magazine at Portsmouth and make Stanstead his base while doing so. As he would be coming through Chichester the city council decided to prepare a pleasant party for him. A handsome quilt was borrowed from Sir John Miller to cover the great table in the Council House and cushions were begged from the cathedral for the benches that surrounded it. The city records relate that 'a dessert of sweetmeats with a bottle of sack and two dozen bottles of the best red and white wine was made ready for His Highness's refreshment.'

The aldermen and councillors in their robes gathered at Sir John's house in Eastgate at 2pm to greet the prince and an elegant speech of welcome had been prepared for the occasion. They waited and waited - but the speech was never delivered. The prince arrived after dark and, without pausing to acknowledge the welcoming committee, rode straight on to Stanstead.

King George I much preferred being in Hanover to England in spite of the scandal of his broken marriage to Sophia Dorothea, which was then the talk of all the courts of Europe. After the birth of their two children George had openly taken a mistress and his wife had embarked on a romantic affair with a Swedish soldier, Count Philip von Konigsmark. But the couple were discovered in each other's arms, Konigsmark was killed, Sophia divorced and kept a virtual prisoner in a castle at Celle in Brunswick for the last thirty two years of her life.

It was on his return from a trip to Hanover in January, 1725 that he made his unintentional visit to Sussex. Bad weather drove his ship into Rye Bay and, as she was in danger of breaking up, the king was put ashore a little to the west of Jury's Gap. He was met on his long and exhausting walk to Rye by the mayor,

The Ancient Town of Rye had an unexpected royal visitor when George I was shipwrecked on his way back from Hanover.

James Lamb, accompanied by the jurats of the town, and escorted to Lamb House where the mayor had his own room prepared for the royal castaway.

This involved moving Mrs Lamb, who was in bed awaiting the imminent arrival of a baby, to another part of the house where she was shortly afterwards safely delivered of a son. The king promised to be a godfather to the child, and as a heavy fall of snow prevented him travelling to London, the christening was hastily arranged.

It was held in Rye Church on January 5 and the royal godchild, naturally named George, was presented with a silvered bowl inscribed: 'The gift of His Majesty, King George, to his godson, George Lambe, Anno Dom. 1725.' Years later, when this bowl came up for sale, it was found to be plated rather than of solid silver.

By January 7 the weather had improved enough for the king to leave Rye and the townspeople packed into what is now the High Street - it was then Longer Street - to say goodbye to him. The trained band with their muskets lined the street and fired a farewell salute which was echoed by the cannon from the Gun Garden. Bells rang out from the church tower above which flew a large naval flag.

TWO years after his escape from shipwreck King George died and was succeeded by his son. George II also preferred being in Hanover but he could at least speak English and would occasionally visit his friends in the country, among them Sir John Lade, whom he created a baronet in 1730.

He came down once or twice to shoot duck at Warbleton, staying with Sir John at Cralle Place. He also intended to visit Eastbourne and the state bedroom at Compton Place was prepared for him by Speaker of the House of Commons, Spencer Compton, but there was a change in the arrangements and he did not turn up.

GEORGE III, who came to the throne in 1760, had been born in England and was proud of it. In his first speech to Parliament he said he 'gloried in the name of Briton' and, unlike his father and grandfather, went rarely to Hanover. He did not come to Sussex either, preferring to visit Weymouth in Dorset for family holidays with his queen, Charlotte. He did, however, recommend the county to a number of his close relatives and sent some of his fifteen children here.

First to arrive was the king's brother, William Henry, Duke of Gloucester and Edinburgh. He came to Brighton, where a season of a sort had been in progress for about fifteen years, on July 11, 1765, and entered immediately into a round of breakfasts, banquets and balls. On his first evening he went to the public rooms to see and to be seen and the next morning he breakfasted at Stanmer with Sir Thomas Pelham who had arranged for 'an excellent band of music, artfully stationed' to play royal salutes from concealed vantage points as the duke strolled round the park.

The royal visitor gave a ball at Samuel Shergold's Castle assembly rooms in the evening, and it was attended by 'a brilliant company of some 250 ladies and gentlemen'. On Saturday morning he drove over to breakfast at the Friars in Lewes with Sir Henry Poole, Commissioner of Excise and Paymaster of Exchequer Bills, and arranged for his host to dine with him in Brighton that evening.

The duke returned to Brighton in an open phaeton and drove around the town to give the people a chance to see him. To be sure he was noticed he had arranged for six young men to run before his carriage and he paid them handsomely for their exertions. He did his share of sightseeing in the neighbourhood and liked Rottingdean so much that he visited it twice.

Another brother, Henry, Duke of Cumberland, then twenty six, and just married to a twenty eight year old widow, Anne Horton, much to the annoyance of the king who; as a result, persuaded Parliament to introduce the Royal Marriage Act, came to Brighton in 1771 and the townspeople greeted him with the ringing of church bells, salutes from the guns of the fort and ships lying at anchor, and a splendid display of fireworks and illuminations. He came back the following year for another week, and between 1779 and 1784 he and his duchess made regular annual visits.

They were always welcomed with great displays of loyalty and affection. The 'running footmen' type of escort introduced by the Duke of Gloucester had caught on and every time a royal coach arrived at the Brighton boundary there would be a team of young men waiting to run before it on its way to the Steine. They were 'dressed in white and made a very decent appearance' when they escorted the seventy two year old Princess Amelia from Stanmer, where she had been staying with the Pelhams, to Brighton in August 1782.

Whether she appreciated such an escort is doubtful. The king's sister was a tough old party who liked to wear men's clothes, take snuff and gamble the nights away. She inspected the horses in her stables every day and had the odd habit of never getting into or out of her carriage at the front door of her house but always in the back yard.

Her visit to Brighton was marred by a tragic accident. The head gunner of the battery firing the royal salute had one of his hands so badly injured when one of the guns misfired that it had to be amputated. A year later there was a similar, but this time fatal accident, when the guns were fired to greet the arrival of the heir to the throne, George, Prince of Wales.

The Sussex Weekly Advertiser reported all the macabre details of the incident: 'About half after two His Royal Highness's arrival was announced by the ringing of bells and a royal salute from the guns of the battery, when unhappily, thro' some indiscretion in re-loading one of the pieces, it went off and wounded the under-gunner so mortally that he died a very short time afterwards. His body was blown off the battery to some distance on the beach, and one of his arms shattered to pieces, the middle part of which was taken up; but his hand, it is supposed, was blown into the sea, as it could not be found.'

Four of the younger children of King George and Queen Charlotte were sent to a much quieter place than Brighton for their summer holidays. In 1780 Eastbourne was a wealthy agricultural parish with a trading hamlet called Sea Houses on the beach. Here some of the warehouses, stores and mills had been converted into substantial residences for the local merchants and it was to these houses that the royal party came.

Twelve year old Prince Edward, later Duke of Kent and father of Queen Victoria, stayed with his tutors at the Round House, which had been built as a flour mill by Thomas Mortimer in 1757. Princess Elizabeth, aged ten, Princess Sophia, two and a quarter, and fifteen month old Prince Octavius and their attendants were at the Great House, which lived up to its name by having five sitting rooms and sixteen bedrooms. It was pulled down in 1830 and the Albion Hotel built on the site. Lady Caroline Finch, governess to Princess Elizabeth and in charge of the party, stayed at Mr James Royer's house, New Susans, later called the Elms, in Seaside Road.

The royal children had an escort of cheering townspeople from Hailsham Common and their arrival, it is said, was celebrated with beer and punch. The way they spent their days by the seaside can be gathered from the 'unpublished diary of a lady' quoted by George Chambers in his *East Bourn Memories* of 1910.

The day the unnamed royal attendant describes is July 7, 1780. 'Rise early,' she writes. 'I sleep in the room with the Princess Elizabeth. After HRH and Princess Sophia and Prince Octavius have bathed, which depends on the tides, we walk on the sands for an hour. Then breakfast. At nine the coach is at the door. We go to Lady Charlotte Finch's house who goes with us to Eastbourne Place, belonging to Lady Betty Compton. . . We stay an hour and Lady C.F. accompanies Princess Elizabeth to the Sea House who then reads the Psalms and chapters of the day, and attends to various lessons from Lady C and myself in ye absence

The Round House where Prince Edward stayed with his tutors and, below, the Great House where the rest of the royal children were accommodated.. It was demolished in 1830 and the Albion Hotel built on the site.

of her teachers. At one o'clock Lady Charlotte leaves us; returns at three, when Prince Edward, his governor Mr Buggmers (Bruyeres) and sub governors Mr Farhill and the Rev Mr Fisher come to dinner. His RH and the gentlemen go away at five.'

The royal children were taken to East Dean and Birling Gap, to Pevensey and Herstmonceux. They used Mrs Webb's sea water baths, which were near the present Leaf Hall, and received seven parcels of fruit every day 'with pigeons and everything I can send them' from Robert Gibbs, agent to the Duchess of Beaufort, Lady Betty Compton's grandmother.

These Hanoverian princes and princesses were far too young to make much of an impression on the Eastbourne social scene but along the coast at Brighton it was a different matter.

# 8

# ROYAL RESIDENTS

## Regency Brighton

IT was on a Sunday in September 1783, a few weeks after his twenty first birthday, that George, Prince of Wales, drove down to Brighton to visit his uncle, the Duke of Cumberland, at Grove House, the red brick mansion overlooking the Steine he had leased for several summers.

News of the fatal accident at the battery when the welcoming salute was fired was not allowed to dampen the royal spirits; however the duke, when he heard about it, immediately made arrangements for the care of the under-gunner's widow.

The prince entered wholeheartedly into the fashionable life of Brighton on his eleven day holiday. He rode out with the staghounds, bathed in the sea, danced various measures at the Old Ship and the Castle Rooms and went twice to the theatre, which was then in North Street.

One morning he and the duke saw from a window in Grove House a coach driven by the Honourable Thomas Onslow scrape against one of the gates. They jokingly criticised his driving and Onslow immediately wagered them ten guineas that he would drive a phaeton and four horses through the gates twenty times at the gallop and not touch them.

This he did, encouraged by the cheers of the townspeople who had gathered to watch, and the royal gamblers paid up. Thomas Onslow's triumph was celebrated in a local rhyme of the time:

'What can Tommy Onslow do ?
He can drive a coach and two.
Tommy Onslow can do more
He can drive a coach and four.'

The prince was also a skilled coachman and, having found

Brighton so much to his liking, he would often drive a three-in-line phaeton down to the coast, attended only by an equerry and a postillion. On one of these visits he had to rush back to London, which he did on horseback, leaving at 5am and returning to Brighton at 10pm the same day, but not on the same horse, having travelled 108 miles and spent a total of ten hours in the saddle.

In 1785 he leased Brighton House in the Steine from the Member of Parliament for Lewes, Mr Thomas Kemp. Later he negotiated through his steward, Louis Weltje, to buy it and he spent the next thirty five years, and a fortune, turning a Sussex farmhouse into minareted marvel of Moorish-style architecture.

He first engaged Henry Holland to convert it into a marine pavilion. New wings were added and the whole of the first floor given over to bedrooms, each of which had a view of the sea. All this work, on which 150 men were engaged, cost money and the prince was soon up to, and over, his ears in debt. He owed £10,000 to a Mr Aaron and another of his creditors sent the bailiffs round to Carlton House, his London home, to recover £600. Fortunately he had some rich friends with him at the time and they paid off the bailiffs before they could seize some priceless works of art.

When all attempts to get his father to help him out of his financial troubles failed Prince George decided to make some drastic economies - and to be seen to be doing so. In May 1786 he sold Carlton House, dismissed his servants and put his stud of racehorses, his carriages and his carriage horses up for auction. Then he travelled to Brighton on the public post chaise to spend the summer quietly by the sea.

With his came Mrs Fitzherbert, a twice widowed Roman Catholic the prince had married secretly six months previously. This marriage was something of an open secret in court circles but it was never publicly confirmed until 1905 when King Edward V11 and Mrs Fitzherbert's descendants made certain documents available for examination.

The prince installed Mrs Fitzherbert in a villa near the Pavilion and mixed hardly at all in society, but by the following summer everything changed. Impressed by the heir apparent's obviously economical life-style Parliament had agreed to pay off his debts and increase his income by £10,000 a year, so he started on the next stage of creating a palace fit for a king-to-be.

He commissioned William Pordern to built the royal stables, now the Dome; and an indoor riding school, now the Corn Exchange. He was so delighted by the Indian style architecture of the stables that he wanted Humphrey Repton to rebuild the Pavilion in that style but he had to wait until 1815, when he was Regent, for John Nash to interpret in stone his dream of a palace of such Oriental splendour that it would be the envy of all the courts of Europe.

Between 1789 and 1793 the social life of Brighton was at its most brilliant. The prince and his companions were there every season, and attracted not only the nobility from all parts of the country but distinguished foreign visitors as well.

Life at the Pavilion, even with the builders in, was lively in the extreme, and it was not any quieter in October 1805 when Mrs

The Prince of Wales dining with friends in the banqueting hall of at the Royal Pavilion. (Picture: Sussex County Magazine)

Creevey wrote to her husband, Thomas, MP for the pocket borough of Thetford and a great gossip: 'Oh, this wicked Pavilion! we were there till half past one this morning, and it has kept me in bed with the headache till 12 today. . . The invitation did not come till 9 o'clock; we went in Lord Thurlow's carriage, and were in fear of being too late; but the Prince did not come out of the dining room till 11. . . I instantly saw that he had got more wine than usual, and it was still more evident that the German baron was extremely drunk. . . The prince led all the party to the table where the maps lie, to see him shoot with an airgun at a target placed at the end of the room. He did it very skilfully, and wanted all the ladies to attempt it. The girls and I excused ourselves on account of our short sight; but Lady Downshire hit a fiddler in the dining room, Miss Johnstone a door and Bloomfield the ceiling. . . At last a waltz was played by the band and the Prince offered to waltz with Miss Johnstone, but very quietly, but once round the table made him giddy so it was proper for his partner to be giddy too; but he cruelly only thought of supporting himself, so she reclined on the Baron.'

Leaders among the noble mischief makers who scandalized half Brighton and fascinated the other half were the Barry brothers. Irish peer, Richard, Earl of Barrymore, who had come in to £24,000 and was not wasting time spending it, was known as Hellgate because of his foul temper. Brother Henry was called Cripplegate because he had a club foot and the Reverend Augustus was known as Newgate as he was constantly in and out of prison for debt.

It was Cripplegate who rode his horse up the stairs and into the attic of Mrs Fitzherbert's house in the Steine - now the YMCA. Two strong blacksmiths had to be brought in to coax the animal down again. Hellgate, in one of his more macabre moods, led a band of so called Merry Mourners round Brighton leaving coffins containing mock corpses outside tradesmens' houses. When the occupants answered a knock at the door they got a nasty shock.

The prince, often accompanied by his royal brothers, the Dukes of York and Clarence, would join the daily promenade on the Steine. The crowd around him was so great that, according to A

Mrs Fitzherbert's villa is in the centre of the houses in the Steine, shown as they were in 1805. It is now the YMCA. (Picture: Sussex County Magazine)

*Stranger's Guide to Brighton* of 1885, he could only be traced by the odour of attar of roses which invariably followed him.

He was a frequent visitor to the races at Brighton and at Lewes, arriving in great style, sometimes resplendent in the uniform of his 10th Light Dragoons and driven by gentleman coachman, Sir John Lade, in a landau drawn by six black horses. He would turn up at the Level to watch the cricket or a prizefight, at the theatre for a play, and to balls at the Castle assembly rooms.

The prince also introduced the public breakfast to the people of Brighton, and they loved it. It was his idea to have an al fresco sort of 'brunch' at around midday at the Promenade Grove in the Pavilion grounds and the Sussex Weekly Advertiser reported on August 12, 1793, that it was 'most elegantly attended by all that is noble, fashionable, or respectable at Brighton and its neighbourhood. . . The wish of everyone present was that of contributing to the general cheerfulness and good humour of the morning, which was remarkably fine.'

The refreshments served included tea, coffee and chocolate,

various fruits and cakes and cold meats, and music was provided by the band of the Surrey Militia. 'The number that honoured His Royal Highness's command was near 400,' says the newspaper, and comments: 'All expressed their entire approbation of this novel species of entertainment at Brighton, and seemed unwilling to leave this enchanting place, as many stayed till near four o'clock.'

For his health's sake the Prince of Wales was advised to take up sea bathing and a local bather, John Miles, generally known as 'Smoaker,' taught him to swim. Smoaker was a blunt elderly Sussex beach boy who spoke his mind even to royal personages. One day, when the prince swam too far out Smoaker called out: 'Mr Prince, Mr Prince, come back' but his royal pupil took no notice. Smoaker dashed into the sea, swam to the prince and pulled him out by the ear. In reply to royal remonstrations about this rough treatment he said: 'I aren't going to let the king hang me for letting the Prince of Wales drown hisself; not I, to please nobody, I tell 'e.'

Smoaker died at the age of seventy four and the prince ordered a sum of money to be given to his widow, so adding just a little more to the new mound of debts he had incurred. He was in the red to the tune of £640,000 and the interest alone on this amount exceeded his income.

This time he found that the only way he could get more money out of Parliament was not only by promising to economise but also by marrying Caroline of Brunswick. On his part his first meeting with his bride-to-be was a case of dislike at first sight, for although she had a pleasant appearance she lacked charm and sophistication and paid scant attention to her personal cleanliness.

He brought her to Brighton in June and they stayed with their suite at Mr Gerald Hamilton's house in the Steine for three weeks while rooms were prepared for them at the Pavilion.

The town put on a great show of welcome for the newly married couple and there were reviews and field days at which the prince's 10th Light Dragoons wore the new uniforms that he had personally designed for them.

Caroline was still in Brighton four months later. The *Sussex Weekly Advertiser* on October 5, 1795 reported: 'Last Wednesday the Princess of Wales took an airing to Copperas Gap and there, attended by Lady Cholmondley, sat under a hedge upwards of two hours where she partook of refreshments, and, being enlivened by the salubrity of the air, seemed to enjoy the rural scene with as much felicity as if she had been sitting under a Canopy of State and feasting on all the luxuries of the East.' Copperas Gap officially became Portslade in 1897.

Caroline left Brighton in November and never returned. But the prince came back. After a few years of domestic difficulties with Caroline they separated and he resumed his relationship with Mrs Fitzherbert and together they mingled with Brighton society once again.

He was then nearing forty and had lost much of the frivolousness of his youth. Although he still pursued a life of pleasure he had a more serious and caring side and this he demonstrated when thirty seven elderly French nuns, who had been driven from their convent at Lisle, were landed on the beach at Shoreham. He sent carriages to bring them to the New Ship inn where he had ordered rooms to be prepared for them, and he and Mrs Fitzherbert collected more than £100 for the refugees and arranged for them to be given sanctuary in a convent in Somerset.

Others fleeing in open boats across the Channel from the terror of the French Revolution also had good reason to be grateful to the prince. The Duchess de Noailles, aged twenty one and very beautiful, escaped from Paris disguised as a boy, crossed the Channel in a storm, and was found by fishermen torn and bleeding on Brighton beach.

They brought her to Mrs Fitzherbert and she was received with 'most polite and cordial hospitality' by His Royal Highness who held a cricket match in the Pavilion grounds for her entertainment, gave a dinner party for her in a marquee on the lawn and ordered his own orchestra to play for her throughout the meal.

Another person to benefit from princely patronage was Phoebe Hessel, a quaint Brighton character with a strange story to tell.

She was born Phoebe Smith in Stepney in March, 1715 and fell in love with a soldier called Sam Golding, a private in Kirke's Lambs. When his regiment was ordered overseas Phoebe put on men's clothes and enlisted in the 5th Regiment of Foot, also destined for the West Indies.

They served and fought side by side for five years and were then posted to Gibraltar, where Sam was injured in action and sent home to Plymouth. Phoebe disclosed the secret of her sex to the wife of the commanding general and she was swiftly discharged and sent home. She nursed Sam back to health, married him, and they lived happily together for twenty years, reportedly having nine children.

Two years after Sam's death Phoebe married a fisherman called William Hessell, but it appears that he was not much of a catch financially. In 1792 their names appear in the Brighton parish book as the recipients of three guineas 'to get their bed and netts which they had pledged to pay Dr Henderson for medicine'.

When William died some Brighton residents clubbed together to buy his widow a donkey so she could hawk fish round the neighbourhood. One day, with her donkey and fish, she stopped for a drink at the Red Lion in Shoreham and heard James Rook boasting of his part in a mail robbery

She reported the conversation to the town constable and Rook and his accomplice, Howell, were arrested, tried, convicted, and hanged at the jail in Horsham.

Phoebe Hessell, a 'jolly old fellow.'

By 1806 Phoebe had established herself as a seller of gingerbread and gewgaws on the corner of Marine Parade, near Old Steine Street. The prince became quite attached to the old character in her black poke bonnet, brown serge dress, white apron and heavy boots and offered her an allowance of a guinea a week. But she would only accept half a guinea - 'it is enough for my needs' she said. In the end he allowed her £18 a year and described her to his friends as 'a jolly old fellow.'

At the age of 107 she attended his coronation celebrations, sharing a carriage with the Vicar of Brighton. When she died a year later her friend, King George IV, ordered a stone to be erected over her grave in St Nicholas churchyard.

By this time his visits to Brighton were getting fewer and fewer, perhaps because of his failing health and the demands of affairs of state. Or perhaps he had lost interest in his Royal Pavilion on which work had at last been completed.

He came down on January 29, 1822, the anniversary of his accession, to open the new carriage road between Middle Street and West Street, the construction of which had been paid for by public subscription. A crowd of 10,000 people cheered him to the echo when he arrived in an open landau accompanied by his brother, the Duke of York; the Duke of Wellington, hero of Waterloo; and the Duke of Dorset.

Like most royal occasions in Brighton the opening of the King's Road went off with a bang, the royal salute being fired from the forty two pounders at the battery and being answered from the revenue cutters, Linnet and Hound, lying off shore.

The king was briefly disconcerted when he found himself being pelted with sugar plums as he drove along the new road. He was not aware of the local 'plums for luck' custom and thought for a moment that his subjects were throwing stones at him. Indeed a rumour to that effect spread round the town and caused no little concern, but this was soon dispelled when several casks of strong beer left over from the coronation celebrations were distributed. The people of Brighton ended up on the beach 'dancing and rejoicing from the base of the cliff to the water's edge.'

That was Prinny's last proper party. The following year he

received Rossini in the music room of the Royal Pavilion on the occasion of the composer's first visit to England.

In 1828 he came to Brighton for the last time and held a Privy Council in the royal palace that had been his playground, and his purpose in life, for more than forty years. . .

# 9

# A PROMENADE OF PRINCESSES

## Beside the seaside

WORTHING'S first chance to play host to royalty came in 1798 when the court physicians advised King George III and Queen Caroline that their fourteen year old daughter, Amelia, might benefit from a course of sea bathing. This tall, pretty, blue eyed, fair haired girl was in poor health and in considerable pain from inflammation of the knee.

Her parents chose the quiet, respectable, coastal town of Worthing where several noble families, deprived of making the Grand Tour because of the unsettled state of Europe, had their summer residences. Princess Amelia arrived on July 31, 1798 with her personal physician, Mr Surgeon Thomas Keate; Lady Charlotte Bellasyse; a nurse, Mrs Cheveley; a deaf governess, Miss Goldsworthy; and her brother, General Goldsworthy, who suffered from apoplectic fits.

They were accommodated in two houses made into one, with Mr Keate and his family two doors away, according to a report in the *Sussex Weekly Advertiser*, which also informed its readers that the princess had the following morning 'much recovered from the fatigue of travelling and is as well as can be expected.'

The exact whereabouts of the two houses is uncertain but 2-6 Montague Place, part of the first terrace of houses to be built in Worthing, has been suggested, as has Bedford House in Bedford Row. For the protection of the royal party in case the disorder in France spread across the Channel, 120 men of the Derbyshire Militia under the command of Captain Shuttleworth pitched their tents beside the houses and out at sea the sloop, Fly, commanded by Captain Cumberland, was on patrol. All pleasure boats were banned from the beach in the interests of security.

The princess's fifteenth birthday on August 7 was celebrated ceremoniously by the army and the navy. The Fly was dressed overall and fired a royal salute which was answered by cannon fire from the militia, which was drawn up on the beach for that purpose.

Amelia was carried down onto the sands on a settee so she could watch the Fly, which sailed close to shore for about two hours, and the militia at drill. After lunch she thanked the gallant captains in person and gave orders for their men to be given bread, cheese and beer.

Peals of church bells were rung throughout the day and in the evening the town was illuminated with coloured lanterns and crowds gathered on the beach to watch a fireworks display from the Fly. Worthing did its best to make Amelia feel welcome and Mr Strynger, a Governor of the Bank of England, who lived in the Summer House between Bath Place and Montague Street, offered her the use of his lawn whenever the tide prevented her from sitting on the beach.

But her brother, George, and sister, Mary, had a poor opinion of the resort. The Prince of Wales often rode over from Brighton to see Amelia and invited her to come back with him and stay in more comfort at his Pavilion. But his mother said no. Queen Charlotte insisted that the lively social scene at Brighton made it no place for an invalid.

Mary, in a letter to the prince, wrote: 'I do believe that, was it not for her own very heavenly disposition, nothing can be more dull than Worthing, or the life she must lead wherever she is, from being quite confined to the couch and suffering so much pain.'

Perhaps it was the quiet life, or the sea air, or a combination of the two, but by November 17 Amelia had recovered sufficiently to go for a three mile ride on horseback and to be driven in a carriage to visit the Duke of Norfolk at Arundel. At the end of the month she was well enough to visit Brighton for the first time. In one of the royal coaches, drawn by four horses, she was driven round the Pavilion and the Steine and along North Street and West Street before returning to Worthing.

On December 7, 1789 Amelia left for London, leaving £20 to be distributed among the poor of the parish of Broadwater and personal gifts for the local people she had employed.

The town soon forgot the pretty princess and all that survives as a record of her visit is a cul-de-sac at the back of Park Crescent called Amelia Road and a pair of pale blue slippers patterned with black and white lines and dots. These are kept in the town museum, but are not often on display.

THE next princess to come to the seaside was eleven year old Charlotte, the only child of the Prince of Wales and Princess Caroline of Brunswick. Her parents virtually separated shortly after her birth and she was brought up by a team of governesses headed by Lady de Clifford.

Unlike her aunt, Princess Amelia, she was a healthy, plump child and a bit of a tomboy, although she could behave with royal decorum when she had to. It must have required all her self control to stop laughing when she visited Worthing's new theatre in Ann Street and heard herself being addressed from the stage by comedian, William Oxberry, as 'royal sweet blossom.'

Much more to her liking would have been the cavalry escort provided by a troop of yeomanry with which she was met at

Findon in July, 1807, and the companies of Volunteers, with their bands, which were assembled to welcome her to Worthing and lead her entourage through the gaily decorated streets to Warwick House, where she was to stay for almost a month.

Charlotte was often taken to Brighton to visit her father and on August 12 he came over himself to collect her to accompany him on his birthday parade. Together they reviewed the troops drawn up on the Downs above Brighton and must have presented a pretty picture - he in his diamond studded uniform and she in a simple white dress with a straw hat. Afterwards Charlotte danced on the lawns at the Pavilion with her favourite uncle, the Duke of Clarence, later William IV, before being taken back to Worthing at 6pm by Lady de Clifford.

The following summer Charlotte was at Bognor, which she made her holiday home for the next three years. This small, seaside town which London hatter, Sir Richard Hotham, was trying to turn into a rival to Brighton, and at the same time planning to change its name to Hothamton, had little in the way of a social season to make demands on her time.

The few soldiers stationed there were mostly convalescing from the Portugese campaign so there were no royal salutes, parades and reviews. Instead Charlotte and her attendants lived comfortably with Mrs Willson at Dome House, built by Sir Richard for just such a purpose, and made many friends in the neighbourhood.

Lord and Lady Sudley took her over to Felpham to have tea with the poet, William Hayley, at Turret House, and he commemorated the occasion in verse. He also wrote a short poem which he planned to have printed on a decorated card and give to the princess as a souvenir of her visit to his printer in East Street, Chichester. It should have read:

Princess! who deign'st a Printer's task to view
This card of duty at your feet would fall
Imprest with all the blessings breathed on you
Vain wish! No volume could comprise them all.

but the typesetter made a mistake and put 'my' instead of 'your' before 'feet' in the second line. Hayley had the whole lot reprinted and changed the first line to:

Princess! so kind a printer's task to view. . .

Another of her literary friends, but on a less elevated scale, was Mr Binstead of the local library who took the greatest pains to get her all the books she asked for. With Lord William, the eight year old son of the fourth Duke of Richmond, for company she was allowed to wander the countryside at will. One of her favourite pastimes was driving her pony and cart as fast as she could round Sir Edward Troubridge's paddock.

Charlotte took full advantage of this relaxation of royal protocol and when she was invited aboard a man-of-war which had dropped anchor off Bognor she climbed smartly up the boarding ladder, totally ignoring the chair which had been lowered to lift her from the captain's gig.

In the summer of 1809 it was a more serious and socially conscious thirteen year old who came to Bognor. On this holiday Charlotte devoted a lot of her time to visiting the sick and taking ailing children to the doctor - the same Dr Davis who wrote the *Origin and Description of Bognor or Hothamtom*. On her third and last visit she joined with Dr Davis and Mrs Willson in making plans for the establishment of a school by the sea for poor children.

In October 1810, to celebrate her grandfather's golden jubilee, this school was set up with the princess as its patroness. Seven years later the Earl of Arran laid the foundation stone for new premises for Mrs Willson's Jubilee School, as it had come to be known. Princess Charlotte was unable to perform the ceremony as she was in the last week of her first pregnancy. She died in childbirth on November 5, 1817.

CHARLOTTE had been married to Leopold of Saxe-Coburg in the hope of securing the Hanoverian succession. With her death that responsibility reverted to the children of George III and a number of royal dukes were rushed to the altar, including the Duke of Kent who married Leopold's sister, Victoria of Saxe-Coburg. In May 1819 they had a daughter, Victoria, and in November of that year one of the baby's four unmarried aunts, fifty one year old Princess Augusta, decided to spend the winter in Worthing.

She was welcomed by the High Constable, Mr Thomas Palmer, at the head of the local militia, and in the evening the streets were illuminated with torches and strings of coloured candle lanterns.

The princess went regularly to what is now St Paul's Church and was then a chapel-of-ease to Broadwater. She was always escorted there by two footmen in powdered wigs and scarlet livery and, with her attendants, occupied three pews which had been specially upholstered in red velour.

There was fairly heavy security surrounding her visit. She stayed at Trafalgar House, later renamed Augusta House, and the town beadle, Samuel Toler, was ordered to be constantly on duty outside it. The town commissioners also had iron lampposts, with extra large lamps, erected round the property, the site of which is now occupied by a multi-storey car park and a block of flats.

There was a good reason for these precautions. The spirit of revolution was abroad all over Europe and in England workers in the industrial Midlands and the north were attacking the new machines which had deprived them of their jobs. In the agricultural south half starved labourers took to rick burning as a form of protest about the pathetic wages they were paid.

# 10

# ROYAL FAMILIES

## William IV and Victoria

WITH the death of George IV on June 26, 1830, an era ended and royal reprobates whose only pursuit was pleasure went out of fashion. The people were no longer prepared to pay for their monarch's self-indulgence when they could not even afford to feed their children. They wanted a responsible and respectable royal family - and got it in the form of William, Duke of Clarence, third son of George III, and his wife, Adelaide of Saxe-Meiningen. He was sixty four when he came to the throne and the ten children he had fathered on the actress, Mrs Jordan, with whom he lived for twenty years, had ceased to be a source of scandal; they were regarded more as youthful wild oats.

William IV was as devoted to Brighton as his brother, George, and presided over lavish state functions at the Pavilion. Mary Frampton, writing in 1831, said that about forty guests were invited each night to dinner, 'realising the entertainments spoken of in the Arabian Nights.' But if there were no guests the king and queen would be quite happy to sit by the fire, he perhaps sleeping in his chair and she doing her needlework, with her attendant ladies also stitching busily.

Typical of this cosy, family scene was the 1832/33 New Year's Eve party at the Pavilion. On the stroke of midnight the guests got up from the card table to bow to the king, kiss the queen's hand and wish them a Happy New Year. 'Let us dance' said the king and Lady Falkland sat down at the piano, everyone took their partners and William led out his old shipmate, Admiral Beauclerk, and they trod a stately measure together.

Charles Greville described the court as 'very active, vulgar and hospitable' with 'King, Queen, Princes, Princesses and bastards constantly trotting about in every direction.'

Active and vulgar it may have been but Queen Adelaide saw to
it that it was also respectable. She would only receive people of
whom she approved and women guests were firmly warned
against wearing the revealing gowns that used to be *de rigeur* in
the days of the Regency. They had to wrap up well, concealing
every bit of skin except hands and face, and hope it would not be
too hot in the banqueting room. She was herself a large lady with
a florid complexion, which is perhaps why she drove daily, when
in Brighton, to drink the waters of the chalybeate spring at Wick.

She exercised a fatal fascination over her chamberlain, Lord
Howe. He was constantly at her side, gazing at her lovingly, to the
amazement and amusement of members of her household. 'This
handsome man of thirty four with a delightful wife was behaving
as a boy in love with this frightful, spotted majesty' wrote Charles
Greville.

William liked nothing better than walking round Brighton and
passing the time of day with whoever he met. And he was
particularly pleasant to children as the Rev Edward Boys Ellman,
Rector of Berwick recalls in his *Recollections of a Sussex Parson,*
published in 1912. 'While I was with Dr Proctor at Brighton I
used frequently to meet King William driving along the front of
the sea and used to delight in the king returning my bow,' he
wrote. 'It must have been very troublesome to the old king to be
continually doing so when out for a drive.'

Another of the rector's recollections reveals that the king could
display unexpected shrewdness. When 'a poor man near Brighton'
sent him a prize turnip he thanked the man graciously and sent
him a guinea. 'Hearing this an individual (whose descendants are
living so I leave out the name) bought and sent King William a
beautiful and valuable horse. The king accepted, and immediately
sent the huge turnip in return, saying the horse was so fine that
he must give something in return that was equally fine of its
kind.'

The king had a great affection for the Chain Pier which he said
reminded him of the deck of a ship. He went on it for the first time
when he was Duke of Clarence and returning in an Admiralty
yacht from Dieppe. He and the duchess received the usual

Brighton welcomed William IV and Queen Adelaide with an arch of evergreens, blossoms and bunting. (Picture: Brighton Royal Pavilion and Art Gallery)

enthusiastic Brighton welcome as they climbed up the ladder on the eastern side of the pier.

The frigate Hyperion was in attendance and fired a royal salute and a huge crowd of onlookers watched as Lieutenant Williams RN, with sailors carrying lanterns, escorted them along the pier deck through a guard of honour of Royal Marines. The band played the National Anthem and Rule Britannia and the Hyperion, illuminated overall, fired rockets into the sky as the duke and duchess walked to the York Hotel where they were received by the Dowager Marchioness of Downshire, Lady Mary Hill, and Mrs Fitzherbert.

Bluff sailor he may have been but King William was also a kind and sensitive man. He showed every consideration to Mrs Fitzherbert and invited her frequently to the Pavilion. Only the Duke of Wellington, who was against the idea, prevented him making a public announcement about her marriage to his brother when Prince of Wales, and he offered her the title of duchess, which she refused. She did, however, go into royal mourning when George IV died and dressed her servants in royal livery. She remained a devout Roman Catholic, in spite of three husbands, and went regularly to confession every Saturday evening at St John the Baptist Church in Kemp Town until her death in 1837. A monument to her, in the form of a kneeling figure with three wedding rings on the fingers of the left hand, is in this church

William did not forget old friends. He had been best man at the wedding of Captain Nelson to Mrs Nisbet in the West Indies and kept up a correspondence with this famous sailor for twenty years. When Nelson's widow, then Viscountess Bronte, was staying at the Sea House Hotel, the king called, without any ceremony, and stayed chatting with her in the coffee room for three quarters of an hour.

But he and the queen could cope quite happily with royal ceremonial when they had to. And there was plenty of it when they visited Lewes on October 22, 1830, to lunch at the Friars, with members of the council. The road from Brighton was decorated with flowers, streamers and evergreens and people attending the quarter sessions from other parts of the county joined the welcoming crowd, as the court sitting was adjourned for that day until 4pm.

Hundreds of schoolchildren were assembled at the entrance to the town from midday onwards and members of local societies lined each side of the road from St Anne's Church to the Friars - a house at the bottom of School Hill which was demolished in 1845 to make way for the railway. It belonged to Nehemiah Wimble, an ironmonger who was a Headborough of Lewes from 1820 to 1831.

The royal salute was fired from the cannon on Brack Mount as the Union Jack was unfurled on the castle. Royal standards were hoisted on the County Hall, the Market Tower and the Friars and Sir John Shelley, MP, with the chief magistrates and town constables, rode out to greet the royal party.

William brought along two members of his family who had been staying at the Pavilion - his sister, Princess Augusta, who had spent the previous winter in Worthing; and his younger brother, Adolphus, Duke of Cambridge.

After lunch Dr Gideon Mantell, the eminent geologist, presented a copy of his *History of Lewes* to the king and the royal party

The Friars, Lewes, where King William IV had an excellent buffet lunch. (Picture: Sussex County Magazine)

visited the castle, the infants' school and the county hall. Before leaving the king wanted to confer a knighthood on his host but Nehemiah Wimble asked to be excused the honour, saying that he wished to die 'plain Mr Wimble'.

He did, however, accept as an augmentation to his coat of arms, the lion of England. Such augmentations were in the personal gift of the sovereign and were usually for acts of bravery or for outstanding deeds. The Earl of Surrey received one at Flodden, the Duke of Marlborough at Blenheim and Nelson at the Battle of the Nile and, posthumously, after Trafalgar. Perhaps on this occasion the sovereign had enjoyed an outstanding buffet lunch.

The visit to Lewes was recorded for posterity by Royal Academician Archibald Archer who spent two years painting accurate portraits of the Lewes and county notables attending the king in front of the Friars. This ten foot by eight foot oil painting hangs, with a numbered key to the people it portrays, in the assembly room of Lewes Town Hall. A similar scene was painted by watercolourist Thomas Henwood and shows the procession of carriages descending School Hill and cheering citizens on the roof top of what is now the National Westminster Bank.

The coat of arms of Nehemiah Wimble, augmented with the lion of England.

Other souvenirs of the occasion survive. Among the Corporation plate is the King William Cup, purchased from the fund raised for the reception of the sovereign, and in Anne of Cleves Museum in Southover is the Royal Worcester tea and coffee service Nehemiah

Wimble had made to commemorate the honour conferred on him. His coat of arms, with its augmentation, is on the plates and saucers. Gideon Mantell recorded the visit for posterity in a pamphlet published the following year. What most impressed him about it was 'the entire absence of the military,' from the day's proceedings.

'With the exception of Colonel Downman, C.B., of Laughton, near Lewes, aide-de-camp to His Majesty (but who attended on this occasion as a country gentleman,) not an officer nor soldier was seen in Lewes, during their Majesties' visit,' he writes.

Queen Adelaide continued to come to Sussex after the death of King William in June, 1837. She spent the first winter of her widowhood at St Leonards, staying at 23 Grand Parade, which was afterwards called Adelaide House. Today it has been divided into flats but still proudly wears a wall plaque, put up by Hastings Borough Council to commemorate the royal visit.

In 1849 the widowed queen brought her entire household to the seaside and took forty rooms for a fortnight at Worthing's largest hotel, the Sea House, which then became known as the Royal Sea House and later the Royal Hotel. It was destroyed by fire in 1901.

THE Hanovers' habit of sending their children to the Sussex seaside was continued by the Duchess of Kent, the widowed mother of Princess Victoria. She personally directed the upbringing of her daughter, who was well protected from the outside world, but when she accompanied her child on visits, at home or abroad, they were almost royal progresses.

On November 3, 1834, the duchess and the princess came by coach from Tunbridge Wells to St Leonards, stopping on the way to have lunch at Battle Abbey, then the home of Sussex MP, Sir Geoffrey Vassall Webster.

The fourteen year old princess describes the whole day in her journal. She writes simply about the things that strike her, such as the portraits of Charles II, William III and Queen Anne at Battle Abbey as well as one of the Emperor Napoleon - 'not full length, but only to the waist; which is said to be very like' - and goes on to describe how it feels to be on the receiving end of a right royal reception:

'The outside of the Abbey is very fine. We left it at half past one. The tenants again accompanied us to Broadslowe (now Baldslow). There some gentlemen from Hastings met us and accompanied us to St Leonards. We passed under an arch formed of laurels and decorated with flowers and inscriptions. As soon as we passed the second arch the mayor got out of his carriage and came to our door asking leave to precede us in his carriage. An immense concourse of people walking with the carriage. The mayor and aldermen preceding us in carriages as also a band of music.

'Throughout Hastings the houses were decorated with flowers and laurels. Ladies and children waving handkerchiefs and laurels on the balconies and at the windows. Cries of "Welcome, welcome, Royal visitors" were constantly heard. We reached Hastings at half past two, and it was four o'clock before we arrived at our house in St Leonards. It was indeed a most splendid reception. We stepped out on the balcony and were loudly cheered. 'One sight was extremely pretty. Six fishermen in rough blue jackets, red caps and coarse white aprons, preceded by a band, bore a basket ornamented with flowers, full of fish as a present for us.'

The princess was delighted to find that her King Charles spaniel, Dash, which had been sent on ahead, was 'in perfect health'. But a few days later both dog and mistress had a narrow escape from serious injury.

They were driving with the Duchess of Kent; Fraulein Louise Lehzen, Victoria's governess; and her new lady-in-waiting, Lady Flora Hastings, in a landau drawn by two horses, when one horse became entangled in the traces and brought the other one down, where it lay kicking and struggling violently.

The princess described in her journal what happened next: 'Two

No. 57 Marina, where the Duchess of Kent and Princess Victoria stayed, was afterwards called
Victoria House and finally Crown House, the name by which it is known today.

gentlemen very civilly came and held the horse's head down while
we all got out as fast as possible. I called for poor dear little Dashy
who was in the rumble; Wood (our footman) took him down and I
ran on with him in my arms calling Mamma to follow, Lehzen and
Lady Flora followed us also. They then cut the traces, the horse
still struggling violently. The other horse, which had been quite
quiet, being frightened by the other's kicking, backed and fell over
into a foundation pit, while Wood held him, and he (Wood) with
difficulty prevented himself from falling; the horse recovering
himself ran after us and we instantly ran behind a low stone wall;
but the horse went along the road, and a workman took him and
gave him to Wood. The other horse had ceased kicking and got up.

'We ought to be most grateful to Almighty God for His merciful
providence in thus preserving us, for it was a very narrow escape.

Both Wood and Bacleberry behaved very well indeed. The names of the two gentlemen who held the horse's head are Rev Mr Gould and Mr Peckham Micklethwaite. The latter I am sorry to say was hurt, but not very materially. The poor horse is cut from head to foot; but the other is not at all hurt only very much frightened. We walked home. . .'

Four years later the bravery of Mr Micklethwaite was rewarded with a baronetcy. Presumably Mr Gould was expected to get his reward in heaven.

After this accident the princess complained of back ache and feeling  sick, but she was not constantly indisposed for she was able to drive over to Bexhill for a meet of Mr Arthur Brooks Harriers. She rode on Pevensey marshes after hounds and a hare was killed within the borough boundary. She must have found it a memorable day for a year later she presented Mr Brook's son, Arthur Sawyer, who succeeded to the mastership, with a silver hunting horn.

Another sport in which she took an interest was archery. She became patron of the newly formed Society of St Leonards Archers, and designed a banner for it, which was presented to the society by her mother. When she became queen she continued her patronage and the name of the society was changed to the Queen's Royal St Leonards Archers.

The following year the princess and her mother stayed for two nights at Buxted Park with Lord Liverpool, whose daughter, Lady Catherine Jenkinson was Lady of the Bedchamber to the duchess. Perhaps it was on this occasion that they visited Lewes Hunt Races and were spotted by the Rector of Berwick, the Rev Edward Boys Ellman. His father had entered a horse which won its race and the princess was asked to present the prize of a silver bowl.

'Princess Victoria was evidently very nervous and wanted to escape doing it,' he writes in his *Recollections*. 'But I heard the Duchess of Kent say that she must. In handing my father the bowl she said: "Mr Ellman, I have great pleasure in presenting you this," and if I recollect rightly did not say much more. My father, on receiving the bowl, seeing the Princess's nervousness and being always ready to talk, in order to put her at her ease, framed his answer in a way in which she had never been addressed before or since, and which evidently amused and took away her nervousness.'

It was almost four months after her accession that Victoria came to Brighton for the first time. The town expected her to love it as it loved her. 'Brighton at this delightful season has particular charm' said the *Brighton Herald* in a leading article. 'The Royal residence is replete with comfort as well as luxury, which is more than can be said of many other magnificent buildings.

'The proximity of the town to London will enable Her Majesty to reside here without inconvenience to her Ministers or disparagement to the business of the country; and we, therefore, look forward with confidence and pleasure to the period when Brighton will have the supreme happiness of ranking among its residents the youthful Queen of England.'

But this confidence was misplaced. After a few visits the queen decided that Brighton was not for her. She wrote in her journal: 'The Pavilion is a strange Chinese looking thing haunted by ghosts best forgotten. I only see a little morsel of sea from one of my sitting room windows.' When walking on the sea front she found herself 'mobbed by all the shopboys in the town, who ran and looked under my bonnet, treating us just as they do the band when it goes on parade.'

Between 1847 and 1848 she has 143 vanloads of furniture, fixtures and fittings, as well as porcelain, carpets and clocks removed to Buckingham Palace, Kensington Palace and Windsor Castle. The Pavilion was virtually gutted and the servants, many of whom had worked there for between twenty and thirty years, were dismissed.

Two years later she sold the once royal palace and its gardens to the Brighton Commissioners for £53,000, but did have the grace, when it was restored by them in 1864, to return some of the original decorations.

But the people of Brighton knew nothing of this on October 4, 1837, when they mounted the most splendid welcome they had ever accorded to a sovereign.

An amphitheatre, 240 feet in circumference and surrounded by galleries which could accommodate more than 2,000 people, was constructed at the bottom of Church Street. These galleries were separated by pillars covered with evergreens shaped like the minarets of the Pavilion and the compartments so formed were hung with crimson cloth bearing the initals VR.

The amphitheatre itself was edged with evergreens supplied by local landowners, including ten waggonloads from Arundel Castle and 7,000 dahlias from a nurseryman at Piltdown. A choir of fifty voices burst into the National Anthem as the royal coach passed beneath an arch of foliage and flowers erected at the entrance to the town, near what is now Preston Circus, and this was followed by peals of church bells and the firing of royal salutes from the battery. Newspaper reports number the welcoming crowd at around 120,000 and say that in the evening the streets were illuminated by 100,000 lamps.

After receiving the town's loyal address from the High Constable, the queen, who was wearing a green silk dress and a pink bonnet, decided to go for a drive around the town. In a carriage and four, with outriders, and accompanied by her mother and the Duchess of Sutherland, she went along East Street to Kemp Town, then back through the main streets of Brighton, returning to the Pavilion at five o'clock.

That good old collector of tittle tattle, Thomas Creevey, dined at the Pavilion that evening. He described the queen as 'a homely little thing' who 'laughs in real earnest, opening her mouth as wide as it can go, showing not very pretty gums. She eats as heartily as she laughs. I think I may say she gobbles. In the Music Room she sang an aria from an opera by Da Costa in a pure, clear voice.'

During this stay, which lasted four weeks, there were more musical evenings and she went to her uncle's favourite haunt - the Chain Pier - where she saw a display by the coastguards and met the pier's designer and builder, Captain Samuel Browne.

In February, 1842 the court was in Brighton again and the citizens of Sussex had a chance to see Prince Albert for the first

The amphitheatre in Church Street from which 2,000 loyal Brightonians welcomed their young queen on her first visit in October 1837. (Picture: Royal Pavilion and Art Gallery

time. Every excursion by the royal party had the municipal
authorities of the towns on its route in a patriotic tizzy. Mayors
queued up to present loyal addresses whenever the royal coach
stopped to change horses, and streets were lined with flag waving
schoolchildren.

The moment they learned that the queen and Prince Albert
would be passing through the town on their way to Portsmouth
the people of Worthing had a meeting to decide how best to
demonstrate their loyalty. They agreed that a cavalcade of
horsemen wearing white favours should meet the royal coach at
the eastern boundary and escort it to Broadwater Green and that
Chapel Road and South Street should be lined with schoolchildren 'to give a more orderly appearance to the streets.'

Contemporary newspaper reports detail every minute of the
brief visit. When the great day arrived 'early in the morning a
comparatively large concourse of persons, both residents and
non-residents, assembled in the neighbourhood of the Marine
Hotel. About half past eight the approach of Her Majesty was

The Marine Hotel, Worthing, scene of an enthusiastic demonstration of loyalty when the royal coach
stopped there for a change of horses. (Picture: Sussex County Magazine)

indicated by the arrival of a party of the Scots Greys, and very shortly afterwards, being rather earlier than was anticipated, the Royal suite, accompanied by Her Majesty's bodyguard and a small mounted procession of townspeople wearing white favours, stopped in front of the Marine Hotel to change horses.

'During the few minutes of Her Majesty's stay here the crowd, consisting of persons of all classes and ages - from the highest to the lowest of our population and from the aged of three-score-years-and-ten to the infant in arms - greeted the Sovereign and Her Royal Consort with the most enthusiastic cheers, which were graciously acknowledged by the illustrious pair.

'The Union Jack was hoisted at the Marine Hotel and at the Town Hall, and a long white flag was hung across the road between the Marine and Sea House Hotels inscribed with the words: "Hail! Victoria, Queen!" The national anthem was played by the town band, which was stationed on a platform fronting the Marine Hotel, from the time of the first appearance of the Royal cortege until it left the place.'

When the royal couple arrived at Arundel the mayor and corporation had assembled outside the Norfolk Arms to present an address of welcome. They were all there again the next day when the queen and Prince Albert returned with some relatives who had landed at Portsmouth from Germany, to join the court at the Royal Pavilion. On this occasion the queen got out of the coach while the horses were changed and was 'received with enthusiastic cheers by the inhabitants.'

There was yet another fervent display of love and loyalty by a crowd of some 30,000 Brightonians when, in the following year, the queen and her consort disembarked at the Chain Pier after a state visit to King Louis Phillipe of France. Before they went abroad they had sent their three little children - the Princess Royal, aged three; the Prince of Wales, two; and baby Princess Alice - to Brighton for the sea air and had a room at the Royal Pavilion turned into a nursery for them. There are security bars at its windows to this day.

On their return from France the royal parents were able to spend two days with their children before sailing to Ostend to visit King Leopold of the Belgians. The royal yacht, Victoria and Albert, escorted by French and English warships, was sighted off Portobello at 3pm on September 7, 1843.

It was a calm, sunny afternoon and the vessel was able to drop anchor within a quarter of a mile of the shore, much to the delight of the crowd thronging the sea front. The queen and Prince Albert, accompanied by one of Louis Philippe's sons, the Prince de Joinville, in the uniform of a French Admiral, were rowed to the pierhead in the royal barge, and walked between lines of coastguards and Grenadier guardsmen, to a carriage and four which was waiting to take them to the Pavilion. The queen recorded in her journal that the Prince de Joinville was 'very much struck with the strangeness of the building.'

Two years later Brightonians had their sovereign with them for the last time. The royal family, with a number of relatives, spent a fortnight at the Pavilion and, in spite of the wintry weather, went out daily either riding, walking and even tobogganing, if that is how one can describe the stately sleigh drives in the Steine, which soon became the subject of a number of contemporary engravings.

On February 14, although it was snowing hard, Queen Victoria and Prince Albert drove over to lunch with the Duke of Norfolk at Arundel Castle. The duke was at Worthing to greet his guests and, after the horses pulling the royal coach had been changed in a record seven minutes, he stoically rode alongside their carriage to Arundel, chatting to the queen through the open window until she asked for it to be closed against the cold.

At Castle Goring a troop of the local yeomanry, commanded by Sir George Pechell, was standing by to form a guard of honour and escort the queen to Arundel. Because of the conditions the men and their mounts were allowed to wait under cover and a look-out was posted on the tower with instructions to call out the moment he spotted the royal coach. But the snow was so thick that he did not see it until it was too late. 'The queen has just gone by' he shouted, and Sir George and his company dashed off in an embarrassed pursuit, not catching up with the royal entourage until it had reached the top of Patching Hill.

The royal return from France in 1843. The queen and Prince Albert arrive by barge at the Chain Pier. (Picture: East Sussex County Library)

Winter sports in Brighton with the royal sledge, sent down from Windsor at the queen's command. Prince Albert is driving the queen and Lady Lyttleton, who has the Princess Royal in her arms. (Picture: East Sussex County Library)

The following year, when the royal couple drove over from Osborne on the Isle of Wight for a more formal and longer visit to Henry Charles Howard at Arundel, 13th Duke of Norfolk, the weather was fine but frosty.

They were met at Balls Hut, about four miles west of Arundel, by their host and some of his guests, including the Duke of Wellington, and escorted the rest of the way by a troop of the Arundel and Bramber Yeomanry. The queen wore as black velvet cape trimmed with sable over a lilac dress. Her bonnet was of white silk and her muff of ermine. This she had to remove to accept the mace offered by York Herald, Mr Howard Gibbon, at the entrance to the town. She returned the mace to him and followed the municipal procession along Old Market Street and through an arch of evergreens to the castle entrance. As the duke's flag was lowered and the Union Jack hoisted the words 'Welcome, Victoria and Albert' extended right across the keep, brilliantly illuminated by jets of gas.

The queen and Albert had passed through Chichester on their way to Arundel and the city fathers had hoped to present each of them with an address of welcome. But as in the case of George, Prince of Wales in 1706, this was not to be. The queen made it known that she would find it distasteful to be detained for the reading and reception of addresses in 'so inclement a season.'

However the corporation was determined not to be denied some form of civic celebration and collected a thousand schoolchildren, gave them each a flag and afterwards a piece of plumcake, and stationed them opposite the cathedral, close to the inn where the royal coach's horses were to be changed. All the houses along the route were decorated - some flags had been borrowed from Portsmouth for this purpose - and they were packed with spectators.

As the royal coach pulled up the children cheered and the mayor and corporation, the Bishop of Chichester, the dean and the cathedral clergy appeared as if by magic to pay their respects. They were, it is reported, 'graciously received.'

On April 18, 1861 the city did have an official royal visit, all of its own. The Prince Consort arrived by train from Osborne on the

The scene of the catastrophe at Chichester cathedral when the spire collapsed on its foundations.
(Picture: Illustrated London News)

Isle of Wight, and was driven in a carriage and pair from the station to the cathedral to see for himself the ruins of its 272ft high spire which had collapsed at lunchtime on February 21, forty seven years after its summit had been rebuilt in solid stone. Fortunately the cathedral was empty at the time and the spire crumbled quite gently into a tidy pile of masonry in the interior.

In the last fifty of her sixty glorious years as Queen of England and her Dominions Beyond the Seas, and since 1877, Empress of India, Victoria did not spend any length of time in Sussex. The royal train stopped at Hastings in 1855 just long enough for the mayor to deliver a speedy loyal greeting, but after the death of her beloved Albert the queen became a virtual recluse.

She spent most of her time at Osborne and Windsor, appearing in public only very occasionally. In 1886 she turned down an invitation from Eastbourne to open its new town hall but she did become a subscriber to All Saints Hospital, which was being built in the Meads, giving ten guineas a year in case any member of her household should need treatment there.

# 11

# SOCIETY - AND SEA AIR

## Edward VII, George V

EDWARD, as Prince of Wales and later as king, was a frequent visitor to Sussex, not only to open hospitals and lay foundation stones but for the racing, the shooting and to stay with friends.

He was not here on duty, so to speak, until 1882 when he and Alexandra, the Danish princess he had married in 1863, went to Hastings to open Alexandra Park and on to St Leonards to open a convalescent home for poor children.

It was a visit not without incident. The prince was handed a ceremonial spade by the designer of Alexandra Park, Robert Marnock, to plant an oak tree. He dug into the earth so vigorously that the handle, made of oak from a submerged forest in the area and decorated with silver, broke off. It had to be hastily replaced so Princess Alexandra could plant a beech tree in the park that bears her name.

The next ceremony, or series of ceremonies, was at Eastbourne the following year. Not only did the Prince and Princess of Wales have to open the new Princess Alice Hospital, but also inaugurate two large pumping engines at the Eastbourne Waterworks Company's Bedfordwell depot; open the new seafront road, Western Parade, which later became King Edward's Parade; and visit All Saints children's hospital which was being built in the Meads.

They were taken from place to place in a procession of twenty six carriages escorted by mounted police and a detachment of the 4th Dragoon Guards brought over from Brighton for the occasion. A public lunch at the Floral Hall was followed by tea on the lawns of Compton Place.

The town provided a lavish luncheon of turtle soup and

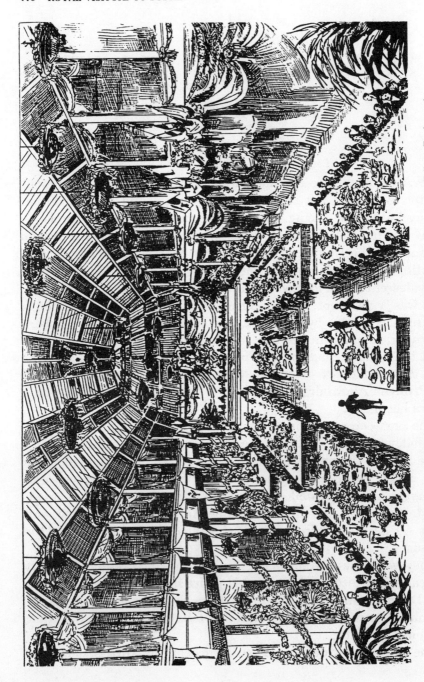

THE ROYAL LUNCHEON AT THE FLORAL HALL, DEVONSHIRE PARK. (Picture: Towner Art Gallery, Eastbourne)

The Prince and Princess of Wales at the opening of the new waterworks in Bedfordwell Road
(Picture: Towner Art Gallery, Eastbourne)

asparagus soup; salmon mayonnaise, lobster salad, pigeon pate, lobster mayonnaise, roast lamb, game pate, turkey, chicken rochet, foie gras, galantine of veal, duckling, beef, chicken with Bechamel sauce, larks in aspic, York ham, ox tongue and quails in aspic. There was Swiss pudding and Charlotte Russe, meringues, strawberry cream, Berlin gateau, orange jelly, fruit salad, apricot compote and baskets of nougats as well as strawberry and pineapple ices, fresh fruit, and biscuits.

The wines to accompany this cold collation were Champagne, Bordeaux, and sherry. There was mineral water for those who wished it.

The hospital which was the prime object of this exercise was a memorial to the prince's sister, Princess Alice, who, after seeing the misery of wounded soldiers in the Austro-Prussian war of 1866, took a great interest in the care of the sick and corresponded regularly with Florence Nightingale.

She came to live in Eastbourne with her husband, the Duke of Saxony and Grand Duke of Hesse-Darmstadt, in 1878, and quickly endeared herself to the townspeople by her very real concern for the aged and infirm. She was only thirty five when she died there of diptheria later the same year.

Another tragic death, this time of the heir presumptive, Prince Albert Victor, Duke of Clarence, a month before his wedding to Princess May of Teck, brought the Prince and Princess of Wales back to Eastbourne in 1892.

The Duke of Devonshire had lent them Compton Place so they could have a few weeks away from the world and a chance to grieve in privacy for their eldest son, known in the family as Prince Eddy, who had died of pneumonia a few days after his twenty eighth birthday. His parents were naturally deeply distressed. The prince sobbed heartbrokenly at the funeral and Princess Alexandra, although consoled somewhat by her deep religious faith, took years to recover from her loss.

With them at Eastbourne for nine days - covering the date planned for her wedding - was Princess May, and they gave her the magnificent diamond necklace they had intended to be her wedding present. A dressing case, ordered by Prince Eddy as his wedding gift, was also waiting for her. 'I remember I felt overcome by this nice thought,' she wrote in her diary fifty one years later.

Prince George, Eddy's younger brother, also joined his parents at Compton Place and went out shopping with Princess May and they played bezique together before and after dinner almost every evening. A year later they were married. . .

It was in his mother's Diamond Jubilee year that the Prince of Wales laid the foundation stone of Christ's Hospital at Horsham. Four years later he was king and one of his first duties in Sussex was to open a sanatorium for consumptives near Midhurst.

For King Edward VII it was more than just a royal opening. The campaign against consumption was one of his chosen charities and he had given the £200,000 he had received for philanthropic purposes from his friend Sir Ernest Cassel, to the sanatorium's building fund.

The ceremony was reported in great detail by the newspapers of the day. 'There was a blaze of waving colour to welcome the King and Queen - a truly admirable assortment floating from every staff, window, turret, tower and tree,' said the *Sussex Daily News* of June 14, 1906. 'At the station, besides a true representation of Sussex nobility, were figures of every branch of Midhurst society, and all of the old town's institutions had adequate delegations. . .

'The Royal train, which had travelled via Dorking, Horsham and Pulborough, reached Midhurst punctually at 4 o'clock. When their Majesties walked from the platform towards their carriage, a reverberating cheer burst from the long lines of spectators. . .

'Members of the Sussex Imperial Yeomanry - fine, stalwart fellows, beautifully mounted - formed a splendid cavalcade. . . He looked "every inch a King" and she the worthiest of 'Queenliest Queens."' It is no wonder that King Edward is popular, admired, beloved; it is not surprising that wherever he goes among his own people and kindred there is a demonstration of affectionate fervour, deafening acclamations and a frantic welcome.'

As prince and as king, Edward had an interest in everything and everybody. 'He has a charm amounting to genius' said one of his sternest critics, Henry Ponsonby.

It was a charm which made him many friends in society and on the fringes of it. He and Alexandra were often guests of American millionaire, Willie James, at West Dean, near Chichester, where the shooting was excellent and bags of 1,000 pheasants a day in November were not unusual. Mrs James was an indefatigable organiser of charity matinees and the king had to give up a day's shooting to go to the Brighton Palladium to watch his hostess play Kitty in a performance of *The Marriage of Kitty*, given in aid of the Queen's Nurses.

From 1903 Edward and Alexandra regularly attended race meetings at Goodwood and everything was done for their creature comforts. Two lavatories where installed in the royal pavilion next to the grandstand, at a cost of £275. The one for the king's use had a monogrammed marble pedestal with a mahogany seat and the handle of the flush pull was silver plated. In the cloakroom to be used by the queen an extra lavatory was installed, as well as an electro plated towel rail and a mahogany shelf with a looking glass above it. Just in case there was not everything to their liking at Goodwood House, where they stayed as guests of the 7th Duke of Richmond for the week's racing, 'numerous dainties for the table' were dispatched from Windsor and some of the queen's favourite pieces of furniture were sent down from Buckingham Palace.

The king was a successful racehorse owner. When he was Prince of Wales his horse, Persimmon, won the 1896 Derby at odds of five to one and in 1909, with Minoru, he became the first reigning monarch to win that race. A few weeks later Minoru won the Sussex Stakes at Goodwood.

The visits to Goodwood were very public occasions and were recorded in full sartorial detail by the local newspapers. The *Chichester Observer* of 1905 told its readers: 'The king wore a grey lounge suit with a light grey bowler hat, looking remarkably well and, as usual, very genial. Queen Alexandra was wearing a lovely dove coloured coat and a toque trimmed with grey and white ostrich feathers and a white stole.'

The king did not like to linger on his way to the races. Chichester's civic leaders, who since the days of George 11 must have become accustomed to their sovereigns sweeping through the city without pausing to listen to loyal addresses, had prepared a written greeting for Edward in 1904. He paused for three minutes by the Market Cross to receive it, and handed the mayor a written reply.

Other visits to Sussex were more informal. The king often stayed with his eldest daughter, the Princess Royal, formerly Princess Louise, and her husband, the Duke of Fife, at 1 Lewes Crescent in Kemp Town, Brighton. He came down for the first time in February 1902 and six years later, while his daughter and son-in-law were away, he borrowed their house for a week to convalesce after a slight illness. On that occasion the other 100 or so families who lived in the Sussex Square area and had a right of entry to the gardens and slopes, were asked by the Kemp Town Enclosures Committee not to use them so that the king could have some seclusion by the sea. They all loyally complied with this request, but the royal invalid did not hide himself away

King Edward VII and the Prince of Wales, later King George V, at Goodwood races in 1909. They are guarded by a sergeant of the West Sussex Constabulary. (Picture: Sussex Police)

totally. He went to St Mark's Church on Sunday and his patronage of local tradesmen resulted in a rash of 'By Appointment' signs appearing on Kemp Town shops.

King Edward also stayed a number of times with his old friend, Arthur Sassoon, who lived in fine style at 8 Kings Gardens, Hove. He did what most holidaymakers do at the seaside when the weather is fine - sit on the sea front, or in the gardens, go on the pier or perhaps visit friends in the neighbourhood.

On one occasion the king was reading his newspaper at the end of Worthing pier when a crowd gathered and he had some difficulty in making his way through the throng to his chocolate brown Daimler which was waiting at the entrance.

However he was not always recognised on these excursions. Worthing pier attendant, George Hunt, had no idea that the elderly gentleman smoking a cigar who inquired of him how to play deck quoits was the King of England. He offered to give him a game. . .

In 1908, after his convalescence in Kemp Town, the king moved along the coast to Worthing and stayed for several weeks at Beach House with Sir Edmund Loder, whose family had lived there since it was built by James Rebecca in 1876.

He liked it so much that he very nearly became a Worthing resident. Just a few weeks before he died, he had started negotiations to buy Beach House from the Loders, who moved the following year to Leonardslee.

On January 12, 1910 the king visited Old Place, Lindfield, the sixteenth century manor house that the eminent Victorian stained glass artist, Charles Eamer Kempe, had so magnificently restored and extended. The king's signature appears in its visitors' book above that of Queen Alexandra, who was at Old Place on May 3, 1914 with a number of royal relatives, including Princess Victoria, grand-daughter of Queen Victoria.

The princess had brought a camera with her and took a number of photographs of the house and its ornate gardens, then the home of Charles Kempe's cousin, Walter Tower and his family.

Ten days later Mr Tower received a letter from Marlborough House enclosing prints of the photographs 'which Her Royal Highness took during her delightful visit with Queen Alexandra to your lovely home.'

Queen Alexandra photographed by Princess Victoria in the garden of Old Place, Lindfield.

(Picture:   Robin Feild)

GEORGE V was forty five when he succeeded his father and Queen Mary was forty three. This somewhat sedate, middleaged couple maintained the disciplined dignity that Queen Victoria had set as a model for the monarchy and there were few scandals, no wild extravagance, and only the mildest of naughty escapades in their court. The king did, however, express himself with nautical vehemence on matters of which he disapproved - as Bognor was to discover.

As a boy of eight Prince George, with his older brother, Prince Eddy, was taken, as their grandmother had been, on holiday to St Leonards. They bathed from the bathing machines on the beach, were taken out in the Hastings lifeboat, the Ellen Goodman, and watched a life saving display by rocket apparatus at Bo Peep.

After that visit Prince George did not come to Sussex for many years. In 1905 he reluctantly agreed to be Lord Warden of the Cinque Ports but refused all requests to perform the duties associated with that office.

The Brotherhood and Guestlings of the Cinque Ports were more than a little upset. They found the prince's attitude 'detrimental to the best interests of the ports' and likely to 'imperil one of the most ancient institutions of the kingdom.' But the prince was not going to be pushed around and in 1907 he resigned.

He did not turn his attention again to Sussex until the 1914-18 war when, at his suggestion, the Royal Pavilion at Brighton was turned into a military hospital where more than 4,000 Indian soldiers were treated for injuries sustained in that conflict.

Operating theatres were set up in rooms in which state receptions had been held, and the extensive kitchens catered for the many different diets required by the religions and castes of the patients. The king, accompanied by Queen Mary and their daughter, Princess Mary, visited the Pavilion in 1917 to see for himself how his idea was working.

King George had inherited his father's love of racing and both as prince and as king he was a regular visitor to Goodwood. It was a few weeks after the Derby of 1913, at which his horse, Anmer, had been brought down by a suffragette, that he arrived at Chichester by train and was the object of another Votes for

Women protest. He was in the station yard inspecting the local division of the National Reserve when a woman in nurse's uniform ran across from the waiting room and tried to give him a petition.

She would have succeeded had not a police inspector intervened and pushed her away. The king's assailant was Nurse Gifford, a follower of Mrs Pankhurst, but no action was taken against her and she was put on a train and sent home to Bexhill.

The next day the king's horse, Brakespear, won the first race at Goodwood but on the whole he was not a lucky owner. In 1923 he wrote ruefully to his host, the Duke of Richmond: 'I am sorry my horses did not distinguish themselves until yesterday when Jass House took it into his head to win.' The queen also wrote to the duke from the royal yacht, Victoria and Albert, at Cowes, giving him a fascinating titbit of news: 'The clergyman at Bosham was seated on the wall of his house when we drove by and I was able to wave him a greeting. . .'

King George's last visit to Goodwood was in 1928 when he caught the chill that led to serious congestion of the lungs. For days he was at death's door but by February 1929 he had recovered sufficiently to go by ambulance to Bognor for an extended convalescence at the home of Sir Arthur du Cros, founder of the Dunlop Rubber Company.

Before taking the tenancy of Craigweil at a nominal rent Queen Mary and her daughter, the Princess Royal, had given the house a thorough inspection. They found that every bedroom had a sea view and the main reception rooms looked onto a terrace and lawn that led to a 200 yard promenade. Seawater was piped to the bathrooms and there was a lift from the ground to the third floor. There was an electric organ in the music room which also had a stage and a film projector. The house was declared suitable and the queen came by car from London on February 9 to await the arrival of her husband.

The king was driven down in an ambulance, the blinds of which were raised, and he managed to smile and wave to the crowds waiting outside the gates of Craigweil. Three days later he was able to smoke a cigarette - the first since his illness - and, on

Queen Mary with the convalescent King George V in the grounds of Craigweil at Bognor. (Picture:
West Sussex County Library)

February 17, when she returned from church at Pagham, the
queen found the invalid taking his first unaided walk.

On Easter Monday the king made his first public appearance,
sitting in a sheltered spot, out of the blustery wind, to listen to the
Kneller Hall band. 'A number of people came up to our sea walk,'
wrote the queen. 'We went and waved to them and there was
great cheering.'

As the king's health improved there was a constant succession
of royal visitors, among them the Prince of Wales, who flew down
in a private plane; the Duke of York; Prince Olaf, later King of
Norway; and three year old Princess Elizabeth. 'George was
delighted to see her,' the queen wrote in her diary. 'I played with
Lilibet in the garden and we made sand pies.'

Now that her husband was better Queen Mary was able visit
the nearby towns in search of antiques, for she was a
knowledgeable and avid collector of pictures and items with a
royal historical interest as well as of jewelled snuff boxes,
miniatures and other desirable little objects.

She went to Wilbury Road, Hove to lunch with Major and Mrs
Woodhouse, the parents of the Marchioness of Dufferin and Ava,
and while there visited the museum and a number of antiques

shops in the Kings Road and Prince Albert Street. Major Woodhouse had a hobby that fascinated the Queen Mary. He made dolls' house furniture for his grandchildren and had a miniature banqueting room on show in London. Some of his pieces were soon in the queen's own dolls' house.

It so happened that Worthing antique dealer Leslie Godden was in Bognor on business on February 27 when the Queen Mary called without warning at his shop in Ann Street. His mother, Mrs Arthur Godden, received the royal customer, who bought a Sheraton card tray and a Sheraton miniature bow fronted chest, before moving on to look at the pictures at Aldridge Brothers art studio in the arcade.

Crowds gathered in Cliffe High Street, Lewes, to see Queen Mary on one of her shopping expeditions. Picture: Sussex Express)

Before the king and queen left for Windsor on May 15 a deputation from the urban district council came to Craigweil to ask if the town could be known as Bognor Regis in future. They made their request to Sir Arthur Stamfordham, the king's private secretary.

He passed it on to his master, who allegedly spoke the famous words: 'Bugger Bognor' in reply, which Sir Arthur tactfully interpreted as the royal assent and informed the waiting councillors accordingly.

Another version of the 'Bugger Bognor' story is that the king uttered the words seven years later, on his deathbed, as one of his doctors, trying to cheer him up, said: 'Your Majesty will soon see Bognor again.'

Two years later there was a great gathering of royalty in Sussex for the wedding at Balcombe of the queen's niece, Lady May Cambridge, to Captain Henry Abel Smith, who had been aide-de-campe to the bride's father, the Earl of Athlone when he was governor general of South Africa. Queen Mary was there together with the Prince of Wales, Prince George, Princess Victoria, Prince and Princess Arthur of Connaught, Princesses Helena Victoria and Marie Louise as well as Princess Sybilla of Saxe Coburg Gotha, Prince Gustav Adolphus and Princess Ingrid of Sweden. There were vast crowds in and around the parish church where the service was conducted by Archbishop W M Carter, formerly Archbishop of Cape Town, assisted by the Bishop of Chichester and the Rector of Balcombe, the Rev D L Secretan.

Before the Silver Jubilee celebrations in June 1935, King George and Queen Mary had a long holiday at Compton Place, Eastbourne. They walked regularly on the promenade and on the beach between the Wish Tower and Holywell when the weather was good, but there were some days when it was too wet and windy for comfort.

On February 27 Queen Mary wrote in her diary: 'An awful night of wind and rain - read and wrote - it cleared up at three and we drove along the esplanade and then to Beachy Head, a nice drive. Walked in the grounds here and actually picked primroses.'

The king went twice to Battle Abbey and called on John Christie

The king and queen take a stroll on the beach towards Holywell during their 1935 holiday in Eastbourne. (Picture: The Sphere)

at Glydnebourne, and the queen visited Sir Paul Latham at his recently restored castle at Herstmonceux, stopping on the way to buy some antiques from Kerridges in Hailsham, which she asked to be delivered to Buckingham Palace. Together they went to Bexhill to see the new pavilion which was being built there, and drove on to the Cooden Beach Hotel, then owned by the De La Warr family, to be entertained by the Earl and Countess.

Preparations were being made for another royal visit to Compton Place in January 1936 but a week or so later came the sad bulletin from the royal physician, Lord Dawson of Penn: 'The King's life is drawing peacefully towards its close.'

In her widowhood Queen Mary made a number of private visits to Sussex, often staying with her sister-in-law, Princess Alice, and the Earl of Athlone at Brantridge Park, Balcombe or with Lady Loder at Leonardslee. She would comb the antique shops for the beautiful things she loved to collect and dealers throughout the county knew her as a most discerning and price conscious customer.

One of her last visits to Sussex was in 1949 when she and the Earl of Athlone spent the afternoon at Wakehurst Place, Ardingly. There she saw the maidenhair tree which she had planted in the grounds of the 16th century mansion owned by Sir Henry and Lady Price in 1927 and, using the same inscribed spade as before, she planted a hybrid magnolia near to it.

# 12

# IN PEACE AND WAR

## The House of Windsor

WITH the accession of Edward, Prince of Wales, the country looked to a new style of monarchy, headed by a young man who had conquered the hearts of the people as their golden boy, their Prince Charming.

By the time he came of age Prince Edward had had enough of his strict upbringing and was ready to enter wholeheartedly into the vibrant social life of the Twenties. He would slip away with Frieda Ward or Thelma Furness, two svelte married ladies with whom his name was romantically linked, for a quiet day by the sea at Brighton. He usually stayed with Sir Sydney Greville, groom in waiting to his father, who had a house in Hove, and sometimes after dinner he would go in an open car to the Palace Pier to see the Follies. Once the prince and his guests walked the entire length of the pier without anyone recognising them, paid for their seats and went into the packed theatre in time to catch the end of the show.

But not all his visits to Brighton were social ones. In February 1921 he unveiled and dedicated the Chattri Memorial to the Indian soldiers who had died of their wounds at the Royal Pavilion when it was a military hospital in the First World War. The small domed monument, designed by Indian architect, E C Henriques, is to this day a place of pilgrimage for visiting Indians and commemorative services are held there.

He had a terrific welcome, particularly from thousands of schoolchildren, at Hastings in 1927 when he opened the White Rock Pavilion. While he was inspecting a parade of ex-servicemen and women arranged by the British Legion he had an unofficial escort - a dog which had been born on the Somme and had been under fire in France, Belgium and Italy.

Down at the Fishmarket, where a triumphal arch had been erected, a presentation was made to the prince on behalf of the town by the oldest fisherman, James Chatfield, and he was also given a golden winkle and sworn in as a member of the famous Winkle Club. This club was formed in 1899 to raise money to help the families of fishermen who had fallen on hard times. Its members would challenge each other with the words: 'Up winkle' and the person so challenged had to produce his winkle emblem or pay a fine.

In June 1931 the prince came by air from Windsor to Eastbourne, landing at the flying ground in Kings Drive at about 11.45am. It was his only official visit to the town and it was a busy one. He was driven in a red Rolls Royce to the Town Hall where he inspected men of the 229 Sussex Field Battery, Royal Artillery; the 5th Cinque Ports Regiment; and the Eastbourne Grammar School Cadet Corps. He laid a wreath at the war memorial and toured the town, visiting two of the corporation's housing estates and the fishing and lifeboat stations as well as planting a tree at the Gilbert recreation ground, afterwards called Princes Park.

There was a civic lunch at the Grand Hotel - the menu included caviar or melon, poached salmon with Mousseline sauce, chicken en cocotte with peas and new potatoes, asparagus, a peach and strawberry pudding and cheese and biscuits - and then it was off to the Princess Alice Hospital to lay the foundation stone of the new wing. After tea at Eastbourne College he flew back to Windsor in his monoplane.

In July the following year the Prince of Wales was at Chailey to open the St George's buildings of the Heritage Craft School for which £25,000 had been raised as a thank offering for his father's recovery from a serious illness in 1929. He was the first person to place a golden apple on the fund raising tree with his personal donation of £50, to which he added a further £500 which had been given to him for charity by a friend.

His next visit to Sussex was one of discovery. He had become interested in gardening and went to Highdown, the chalk garden near Worthing, to seek advice from Lady Stern on what he should

There were some high kicks from this police horse when the prince, in a red Rolls Royce, was driving through an arch of nets to Eastbourne's fishing station. Below: The motor cycle escort provided by Brighton Borough Police when the Prince of Wales came to unveil the Chattri Memorial. (Pictures: Sussex Police)

plant at Fort Belvedere. 'We weeded feverishly for days before the prince arrived,' wrote Lady Stern in her diary. 'During his visit the prince talked incessantly about gardens and gardening personalities and I asked him how long he had been interested in it. He said three months and laughed at his own ignorance and impatience.'

It was soon after this visit that the prince met Mrs Simpson for the first time. It was a meeting which was to have a dramatic affect on English constitutional history for, on December 10, 1936 he renounced the throne because, as king and Defender of the Faith, he could not marry an American woman who had divorced one husband and was divorcing another.

'You must believe me when I tell you that I have found it impossible to carry the heavy burden of responsibility and to discharge my duties as king as I would wish to do without the help and support of the woman I love,' he told the nation in his Abdication broadcast.

A week beforehand, when the British press broke the story which had been headlines in America for months, Mrs Simpson fled to France. She drove down from London to Newhaven with Sir Walter Monkton and a detective. Fortunately for them there were no reporters about and they were able to slip unrecognised aboard the French ferry, the SS Newhaven, at 8pm, two hours before the boat sailed.

Three years later the Duke and Duchess of Windsor were in Sussex again. They had been brought back from France on HMS Kelly, commanded by Lord Louis Mountbatten, nine days after war was declared.

It had been made clear to them that no royal accommodation would be offered so they accepted an invitation to stay with their friends, Major Edward 'Fruity' Metcalfe and his wife, Lady Alexandra, at South Hartfield House, Coleman's Hatch. The Duke of Windsor saw his brother, King George V1, at Buckingham Palace on September 14, and made other journeys to London from Sussex to prepare for the war job he had been offered as liaison officer with the Military Mission in France.

The *Sussex Express and County Herald* of September 15

published a photograph of the duke and duchess sitting in the garden of South Hartfield House. It is accompanied by the guarded statement: 'The Duke and Duchess of Windsor have arrived in England, and are staying in the country until His Royal Highness takes up a war appointment.' They left Sussex, and England on September 29.

GEORGE VI had kingship thrust upon by his brother's abdication. He was a shy and hesitant man and, although schooled to accept royal responsibility, he did not greatly relish doing so suddenly, and in this way. As Duke of York, with his duchess - he had married Lady Elizabeth Bowes-Lyon in 1923 - he had fulfilled all the usual royal duties of overseas tours and of opening this or that when at home.

He was first in Sussex in 1918 when he had just transferred from the Royal Navy to learn to fly with the Royal Air Force. He was stationed for a short time at Hastings with the RAF Cadet Brigade and marched at the head of a column of men when it was inspected by his father, George V.

There was another war raging in May 1940 when, accompanied by Winston Churchill, King George VI was in Brighton to inspect the sea defences. The beaches had been mined, machine gun posts set up and the centre sections of the Palace and West piers had been demolished by the Royal Engineers.

He was at Hove in May of the following year to see the school for naval officers at the King Alfred and to inspect naval cadets at Lancing College and visit a number of the Canadian units stationed in the area. There were no crowds of people waving flags, no welcoming addresses, no triumphal arches on these occasions. . .

Queen Elizabeth also visited Sussex in wartime. She went to Rottingdean to inspect the London Scottish Regiment of which she was honorary colonel and, in the winter of 1939, she went to West Sussex to see the Women's Voluntary Service work with evacuees.

There was an atmosphere of happy informality on this occasion. The royal visitor shared a threepenny canteen lunch with 250 evacuees at Chichester, sitting at a table with some of the

The sun was up and the hood of the royal car was down when the Duke and Duches of York arrived in Eastbourne for a short holiday in 1935. (Picture: Towner Art Gallery)

children; she inspected the canteen kitchens there and at Selsey; and 4,000 youngsters lined the city streets to cheer her as she left. On her way down she had stopped at Bosham to visit its ancient church and when she came out she saw the harbour with the tide in. 'What a grand place this is,' she exclaimed.

Three years earlier, with her husband, then still the Duke of York, and children, she had stayed at Compton Place, Eastbourne to recuperate from bad bout of influenza. The soft strawberry and cream pink of the exterior stonework so impressed her that she had the Royal Lodge at Windsor painted the same colour.

It was a quiet, family holiday with visits to friends in the neighbourhood, to St Mary's  Church in the Old Town on Sundays, and walks on the beach and the Downs.

Since the death of her husband and the accession of her daughter in 1951, Queen Elizabeth, the Queen Mother, has visited the Sussex many times. Like the rest of the royal family she has enjoyed days at the races, particularly at Goodwood, and she takes her duties as Lord Warden of the Cinque Ports very seriously. In that capacity she has visited the Ancient Port of Rye and the Ancient Town of Winchelsea and was at Hastings in May 1986 to open the newly electrified railway line to London.

She has been many times to Chailey Heritage and to Gifford House, the Queen Alexandra Hospital for Disabled Ex-Servicemen in Worthing of which she is president.

Farewell handshake from a future Queen of England for the Rev F P Hughes. Princess Elizabeth and Princess Margaret Rose with their parents outside St Mary's Church in Eastbourne Old Town.

England in wartime and Queen Elizabeth sees for herself how the evacuees have settled in at Horsted Keynes in 1939. (Picture: Mid Sussex Times)

The royal president of the Queen Alexandra Hospital for Disabled Ex-Servicemen with Les Longman, one of the oldest residents of Gifford House in Worthing, and two rather over-awed little girls. (Picture: Worthing Herald)

Smiling through the rain. The Queen Mother, Lord Warden of the Cinque Ports, on an official visit to the Ancient Port of Rye. (Picture: Rye Express)

PRESENT day official royal visits bear little resemblance to the progresses of the past. No longer does the entire court take a holiday and save on the housekeeping by demanding hospitality from the nobility of the shires. Modern royals often undertake lengthy overseas tours to boost Britain and strengthen links with the Commonwealth but home visits tend to last a few hours rather than days.

In recent years the threat of terrorist attack has resulted in a tightening of security around royal personages. Members of the public are usually kept at a safe distance and most ceremonies are ticket only affairs. But still the crowds gather to see the sovereign and members of the royal family as they have done throughout history. It matters not a jot that they are seen almost daily on television and their photographs appear regularly in newspapers - the people want the presence, not the pictures.

Since the 1939-45 war royal visits have tended to follow a set formula. Younger royals drop in by helicopter to fulfil a number of engagements in fairly quick succession - flying away with a smile and a wave around 4pm.

In the early part of her reign, when she had friends living in the county, the queen, with the Duke of Edinburgh, used to stay longer, although her busy schedule of visits, both home and overseas, did not permit the acceptance of too many invitations.

In the 1960s, for instance, they were frequently the guests, first at Uckfield House, Uckfield and then at Horsted Place, near Lewes, of Lord Rupert Nevill, the duke's private secretary, and Lady Nevill.

A typical business and pleasure visit was in July 1962 when they came by road to Uckfield, arriving at 1pm on Saturday, and leaving on the Monday morning for a six and a half hour series of official visits to Lewes, Newhaven, Brighton and Hove.

On the Saturday afternoon the queen went racing at Lingfield Park - it was a sponsored meeting in aid of the British Olympic equestrian team - and the duke drove over to Cowdray to watch the polo. He was there again on the Sunday, after going with the queen and his host and hostess to morning service at Uckfield Parish Church.

These two days of informality were followed by one of ceremonial. The flags were out; the royal route was lined with cheering children; buglers of the Royal Sussex Regiment sounded a fanfare and members of the regiment lined the staircase at Lewes Town Hall where members of the council were presented to Her Majesty. Then it was on to Newhaven to meet the crew of the lifeboat and visit the disabled at the Searchlight Workshops; and to St Dunstans at Ovingdean and the Royal Pavilion at Brighton.

At Hove, her last port of call, the crowd was so great when the queen opened the £12,000 George Street improvement scheme, that the royal Rolls got caught in the crush and she had to wait for it to reach her.

Four years later the queen and duke stayed again with the Nevills before and after a seven hour tour of East Sussex to mark the 900th anniversary of the Battle of Hastings. In a maroon coloured glass-topped Rolls Royce they arrived first at Battle,

The queen has a special smile for her smaller subjects as she leaves Uckfield Parish Church after morning service. (Picture: Sussex Express)

The queen and the duke receive souvenirs of their visit to Lewes in 1979 when they came to open the new training wing of Sussex Police headquarters. (Picture: Sussex Police)

visiting the abbey and the church, and then went on to Rye where the queen renewed acquaintance with a horse she used to own. It was her 1965 Goodwood Cup winner, Augustine, which had been trained at Jack O'Donahue's Reigate stables,where the mayor of Rye's daughter-in-law used to work before her marriage. At Winchelsea there was another link with the past - the queen was presented with a picture of herself taken outside the church there when she visited it with her parents when they were staying at Compton Place, Eastbourne in 1935. At Hastings Prince Philip was made a member of the Winkle Club and given some expert advice about what to eat with the bloaters which he had been given in a Sussex trug at Rye.

At Bexhill - receiving its first official visit by a reigning monarch - the queen toured the De La Warr Pavilion, which had been opened by her parents when Duke and Duchess of York, and was given a basket containing two model corgis made of beech leaves over wire frames.

At Eastbourne there were plaques to be unveiled at Chelsea College of Physical Education and at Eastbourne College, which was preparing for its centenary, before the queen and the duke returned to Horsted Place to which the Nevills had moved a few months earlier. After a short rest there they were driven by Lord Rupert to Uckfield station and, watched by a crowd of about 200 people, they left to travel overnight to Aberfan. They returned from Wales by air to Gatwick on the Saturday and drove back to Horsted Place, where they stayed until Monday.

On those few days in October 1966, Queen Elizabeth II travelled many hundreds of miles, fulfilled many official engagements, gave pleasure to thousands of people and collected a motley assortment of modestly priced gifts.

When Queen Elizabeth I visited East Sussex in 1573 she was here for at least three weeks with her court, which cost the earth to entertain, and went back to London loaded with gold, silver and jewels. Her three day visit to Rye alone cost the town £150, which is about £20,000 in today's monetary terms.

Like her grandfather and her great grandfather the queen is a regular visitor to Goodwood for the race week in July. She has followed the tradition started by Edward VII of holding privy councils in the Tapestry Drawing Room of Goodwood House and from there a number of important decisions of state have been made. But the one that brought Britain to the brink of war with Egypt over Colonel Nasser's seizure of the Suez Canal was taken at Arundel Castle in 1956. That year the queen was the guest of the Duke of Norfolk for Goodwood and, after a quickly convened Privy Council at Arundel, she signed the proclamation calling up the army reservists.

It was an affair of state - the 1983 General Election - that caused her to postpone her promised visit to the South of England Agricultural Show at Ardingly in the year that her lady-in-waiting, the Marchioness of Abergavenny, was the show society's president. She put it off to the following year at the request of the Prime Minister, Margaret Thatcher, who feared the royal presence at Ardingly would keep loyal Sussex voters away from the polls.

It was a ceremony of state - the distribution of the Royal Maundy - which brought her to Chichester Cathedral in 1986.

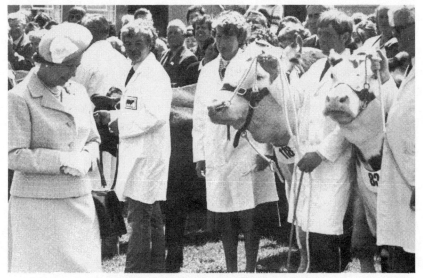

The queen inspects the cattle lines on her 1984 visit to the South of England Show at Ardingly.
(Picture: Sussex Express)

The practice of the monarch washing the feet of the poor to commemorate Christ's washing the feet of his disciples at the Last Supper dates from the conversion of England to Christianity in the sixth century. Still used at the start of the service are His words: 'A new commandment I give unto you; that ye love one another' which, in Latin, begins 'Mandatum novum do vobis' - hence Maundy from Mandatum - a commandment.

Records of the Maundy service go back to the days of Edward I, builder of Winchelsea. It used to be held at the Chapel Royal, Whitehall and then at Westminster Abbey, until the queen decided to move it around the country.

In the days of the first Elizabeth the practice of the sovereign washing of the feet of her subjects still had about another 150 years to run. It was not abolished until around 1730. As Tudor feet were rather smelly the queen ordered the Yeoman of the Laundry to see that the recipients were well scrubbed and rinsed in scented water before being touched by her lips. As a reminder of this practical solution to a problem of personal hygiene the Lord High Almoner and his assistants still have pieces of linen as part of their ceremonial dress for the service and, like the sovereign, they carry nosegays of sweet smelling flowers.

At Chichester thirty men and thirty women received the Royal Maundy, the specially minted two pence, three pence and four pence pieces totalling as many pence as the sovereign's age. She was then sixty.

Had the ceremony been held in the seventeenth century they would have also been given two and a half yards of woollen cloth to make a suit, linen for two shirts, a pair of shoes and stockings, three dishes of fish, a gallon of beer, a quart bottle of wine, and six loaves of bread. Nowadays they get cash in lieu.

They also each get £1, instead of one of them being given the gown the queen is wearing. This gown-giving tradition was started by the ultra devout Queen Mary I - she who ordered the burning of the Lewes martyrs - but discontinued by the more practical, and Protestant, Elizabeth I who instead redeemed the garment with a gift of twenty shillings to each of the recipients of the Royal Maundy.

The queen distributes the Royal Maundy at Chichester Cathedral in 1986.
(Picture: Littlehampton Gazette)

PRINCESS Elizabeth and Princess Margaret spent many holidays in Sussex, either with their parents, the Duke and Duchess of York, or in the care of the royal governess, Miss Marion Crawford. The queen first came to the county at the age of three, when she stayed at Craigweil, near Bognor and did so much to cheer up her grandfather, George V, then recuperating from a serious illness.

In the early 1950s Princess Margaret was a frequent guest of the Hartingtons, heirs to the Duke of Devonshire, at Compton Place, Eastbourne. She also stayed with the Tom Egerton at Mountfield and at Beechwood, the luxurious home near Chichester of American publicist and historian, Herbert Agar, and his wife Barbie, widow of one-time Tory Minister, Captain Euan Wallace. Their son, Billy Wallace, was at that time part of the 'Margaret Set' and there was talk of a royal romance.

But it was more than talk that brought the world's press to Sussex in the last weekend of October 1955. Would she or would she not marry Group Captain Peter Townsend? That is what everyone wanted to know and reporters and photographers converged on Uckfield in an attempt to find out.

Princess Margaret and Group Captain Townsend were the guests of Lord and Lady Rupert Nevill at Uckfield House from the Friday to the Monday - for what turned out to be the end of their romance. On her return to London on October 31, Princess Margaret issued a statement saying that she had decided not to marry him - 'mindful of the Church's teaching that Christian marriage is indissoluble, and conscious of my duty to the Commonwealth.'

Still the fifty strong contingent of pressmen did not go away. They kept up their 6am to midnight vigil on the Nevills' house in Water Tower Lane and attention was focused on every car which came and went through the gates. When Peter Townsend went with Lady Rupert Nevill and her children to visit the Marquess

and Marchioness of Abergavenny at Eridge on the Tuesday after the princess's
announcement, he was trai-
led there and back. He finally
agreed to say a few words - to
the effect that he would never
speak of the romance that
came to nothing, and that he
would be returning to Brus-
sels, where he was air
attache, the following weekend.

While all this was going on
British diplomat Kim Philby
was living quietly at Crow-
borough, midway between Uckfield and Eridge. He had been
named as the Third Man in the Burgess-McLean spy scandal and
the press was desperate for his story. Reporters would converge
on his house around lunchtime, leaving the royal romance for an
hour or so, but they never found him at home. Philby, who spent
the rest of his life in Russia, where he was given the rank of
colonel in the KGB, avoided their attentions by breakfasting early
and spending the day in Ashdown Forest.

Another Princess Margaret romance, and this was one that led
to marriage, has an even closer connection with Sussex. It was
when she was again staying at Uckfield House that she first met
Anthony Armstrong-Jones, who had come down to photograph the
Nevill's children.

In 1967, seven years after their wedding, Lord Snowdon bought
a country cottage, Old House at Handcross, and supervised its
conversion and restoration. He also arranged, and photographed
for the private royal album, the 'opening ceremony' in which the
Queen Mum severed the obligatory white ribbon with an extra
large pair of scissors, watched admiringly by the queen and the
rest of the family.

Princess Margaret had not much enthusiasm for country

cottage life and rarely stayed at Old House although her daughter, Lady Frances Armstrong Jones, was christened at Stapleford church in 1964 and her son David, Viscount Linley, was a boarder at Ashdown House, Forest Row, and she often went to his school sports days.

Her official visits to Sussex, which started when she was seventeen and lunched at the Grand Hotel, Eastbourne with the Dukes of Norfolk, Devonshire and Richmond, are usually connected with an organisation or charity in which she has an interest. Her association with Pilgrims, the school for asthmatics at Seaford, goes back to 1955 when she helped to raise £26,000 to build it by staging the Edgar Wallace thriller, *The Frog*, in London. She attended the school's silver jubilee in 1980, and in April 1987 came down to open a new girls' house in Firle Road.

Princess Margaret watches a young computer enthusiast at work, or perhaps at play, on one of her visits to Pilgrim's School, Seaford. (Picture: Sussex Express)

The flags, and the children, were out to welcome Prince Charles when he came down to see the damage done in Ashdown Forest by the great gale of October 1987. (Picture: Sussex Express)

THE first royal rider to compete in a race on the flat - and very nearly win it - did so at Plumpton in March 1980. Prince Charles, wearing the black and gold colours of American billionaire art collector Paul Mellon, rode Long Wharf into second place in the two mile Madhatters Private Sweepstake, run in aid of the Injured Jockeys' Fund, for which it raised £1,300.

Long Wharf was a hot favourite at 13-8 but was beaten by two lengths by a 14-1 outsider, Classified, ridden by BBC radio sports commentator Derek Thompson. The prince apologised to the crowd from the unsaddling enclosure. 'I enjoyed it but I would like to say how sorry I am to the people who put money on my horse,' he said. 'Next time I shall know what to do and how to catch up with the man in front.'

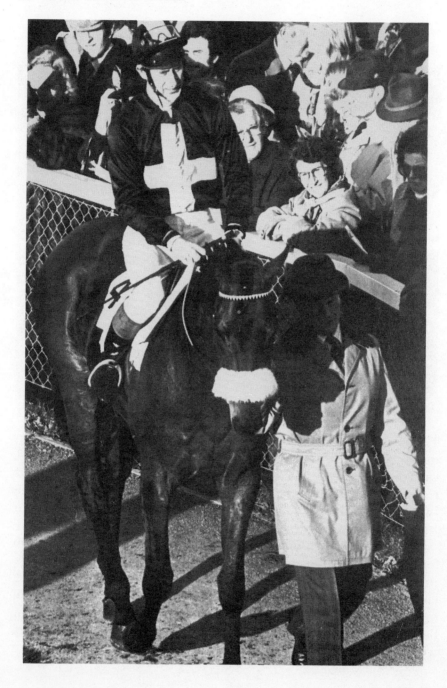

More than 5,000 people had turned up at the picturesque course at Plumpton to see the prince. Every time a helicopter landed by the home turn all eyes were on it to see who would alight but the heir to the throne was already there. He had arrived by car a good hour before the first race and had walked the course with local steward, Derek Wigan, and Long Wharf's trainer, Ian Balding.

Another equestrian sport which has brought him frequently to Sussex is polo which he plays at Cowdray Park. But it is not just for the sport that the prince comes to Sussex. After the great gale of October 16, 1987, when the county lost a large proportion of its woodland, he came to see for himself the damage that had been done in Ashdown Forest and to discuss plans for re-planting.

THE first time the county saw the pretty Princess of Wales in the flesh, so to speak, was in August 1985, four years after her wedding. Wearing the navy blue and red uniform of the Red Cross - she is patron of British Red Cross Youth - she spent nearly three hours at Hindleap Warren, near Chelwood Gate, the London Federation of Boys Clubs' activity centre, meeting and chatting to the thirty handicapped youngsters who were there for a week's activity holiday as guests of the Sussex branch of the British Red Cross Society.

Four months later she delighted the crowds which had gathered to see her by making three informal walkabouts when she was at Burgess Hill to open the Ernest Kleinwort Court, a £75,000 Disabled Housing Trust complex of flats and bedsitters for physically handicapped young people.

The princess is currently top crowd puller among the younger royals, whatever the occasion. Even the opening of the new magistrates court in the county town of Lewes, at which she was surrounded by ceremonial and there was no chance of a walkabout, caused the crowds to gather at every possible vantage point on her route.

In an unscheduled walkabout at Burgess Hill Princess Diana found time for chat with Sister Columba of St George's Retreat. (Picture: Mid Sussex Times)

THE queen and Prince Philip's close friendship with the Nevills resulted in the children of both families becoming friends. Both Princess Anne and Rose Nevill were nine year old bridesmaids at the wedding of Princess Margaret and Anthony Armstrong-Jones and the princess often stayed at Eridge Castle and drove over to play tennis at Uckfield House, which was demolished in 1975 to make way for a housing estate.

Her devoted work for the Save the Children Fund, which has taken her on a number of arduous overseas tours, brought her to Eastbourne in 1977. She was guest of honour at a gala night in aid of the fund. A year later she toured the Hawkins and Tipson factories in Hailsham and received from Jack Hawkins, the chairman of ropemakers, Burfield and Son, a scrambling net for the Oakwood Centre, a Save the Children Fund outdoor adventure and intermediate treatment centre at Burwash.

After lunching at Beacon School, Crowborough on food prepared by four seventeen year old sixth formers - pear and walnut salad, paupiettes of veal, souffle Monte Cristo and petits fours - she opened the school's jubilee sports hall and then went on to Burwash to deliver the scrambling net.

Princess Anne, president of the Save the Children Fund, at Lancing College.
(Picture: Worthing Herald)

GUESTS at the wedding in Uckfield of Buckingham Palace secretary, Sarah Yorke, and banker, Richard Warburton, in April 1988, were surprised to find themselves rubbing shoulders with royalty. The Duke and Duchess of York and Prince Edward were in the congregation at Holy Cross Church and their acceptance of invitations from Mr and Mrs David Yorke to their daughter's wedding - Sarah was secretary to the duke and Prince Edward - was kept a closely guarded secret for security reasons.

After the ceremony the royal visitors joined the 380 guests at the reception given by the bride's parents in the grounds of Holford Manor, North Chailey.

Two years later the duchess, as president of the British Hackney Horse Society, was guest of honour at the South of England Show.

TODAY the pattern of royal visits to Sussex is not unlike that of the medieval period when the monarch came to perform official duties or to take part in sports and pastimes closely associated with the horse. Although the Royal Pavilion at Brighton still retains the splendour that made it the envy of all the courts of Europe no longer  are there any royal residents.

The queen and the Duke of Edinburgh move between Windsor, Sandringham and Balmoral, the Prince of Wales and the Princess Royal have gone to Gloucestershire and the Yorks have built of house in Surrey. Even the private visitsof earlier years have grown fewer as family friends have died or moved away. For the moment it is not Royal Sussex - but 1,500 years of history shows that it has been . . .

# SELECT BIBLIOGRAPHY

Sussex Archeological Collections:
Vol 2. Royal Journeys in Sussex from the Conquest to King Edward I by W H Blaauw
Vol 2. Letters of Edward, Prince of Wales by W H Blaauw
Vol 3. Documents Relating to Knepp Castle
Vol 5. Queen Elizabeth's Visits to Sussex by William Durrant Cooper
Vol 10. Progress of Edward VI in Sussex by J G Nichols
Vol; 25. Sussex Certificates for the Royal Touch by the Rev F H Arnold

**Newspapers and Magazines:**
Brighton and Hove Herald
Chichester Observer
Country Life
Eastbourne Gazette
Eastbourne Herald Chronicle
Evening Argus
Hastings Observer
Mid Sussex Times
Sussex County Magazine
Sussex Daily News
Sussex Express
Sussex Life
Sussex Weekly Advertiser
West Sussex Gazette

**Sussex Books:**
All Saints Hospital, Eastbourne. Denys Giddy
A Peep into the Past. John G Bishop, 1892
Arundel. Borough and Castle. G W Eustace, 1922
Ashburnham Church. Rev J D Bickersteth
Bourne in the Past - Being a History of the Parish of Westbourne   J H Mee, 1913

Brighton Chain Pier. Clifford Musgrave. Leonard Hill (Books)
Brighton Pavilion. John G Bishop, 1903
Brooker's Guide and Directory for Uckfield and District. 1888
Bygone Eastbourne. J.G Wright
Chronicle of Battel Abbey. M A Lower
Cowdray in the Parish of Easebourne. Compiled by Torrens Trotter
Enchanted Forest: The Story of Stansted. The Earl of Bessborough with Clive Aslet. Weidenfeld and Nicholson
Glimpses of Our Sussex Ancestors. C Fleet. 1883
Glimpses of Old Worthing. Edward Snewin
Hailsham and its Environs. Charles Robertson, 1981
Historic Hastings. J Manwaring-Baines, Cinque Ports Press
History of Bognor Regis. Gerard Young. Phillimore, 1983
History of Ditchling. Henry Cheal, 1901
History of Winchelsea. W D Cooper, 1850
King Edward VII Hospital, Midhurst. S E Large. Phillimore
Narrative of the Visit of William IV and Queen Adelaide. Gideon Mantell, 1831
The Old Ship: A Prospect of Brighton. Raymond Flower, 1986
Parry's The Coast of Sussex, 1883
Recollections of a Sussex Parson. Rev Edward Boys Ellman,
Records of Chichester. Compiled by T G Willis, 1928
Strangers Guide to Brighton. W E Nash, 1885
The Story of Bexhill. L J Bailey, 1971
The Victoria History of the County of Sussex. OUP

**General:**
Anglo Saxon Chronicles. Translated and collated by Anne Savage. Papermac 1984
Edward VII, Prince and King. Giles St Aubyn, Collins 1979
History of England and Great Britain. Professor J M D Meiklejohn
King George V. Kenneth Rose. Weidenfeld and Nicholson
Progresses and Public Processions of Queen Elizabeth, John Nichols 1823
Victoria's Travels. David Duff. Frederick Muller

# ILLUSTRATIONS

For the photographs of royal personages that appear in this book I am deeply indebted to the Eastbourne Gazette and Herald Chronicle, the Collection of the late Eric Redfern, the Littlehampton Gazette, the Mid Sussex Times, the Sussex Express and County Herald, and the Worthing Gazette and Herald.
The East Sussex County Library Local Studies Department and the West Sussex, County Library Local Studies, the Brighton Royal Pavilion and Art Gallery, the Towner Art Gallery, Eastbourne, Worthing Museum and T R Beckett Ltd, publishers of the Sussex County Magazine, have kindly given permission for the reproduction of a number of the illustrations in the text, the source of which is indicated in the individual captions.
I am most grateful to Mr Robin Feild for permission to reproduce the photograph of Queen Alexandra on page 123 and to Mr and Mrs Richard Warburton for allowing me to use one their wedding photographs on page 159.
Where no source is indicated the illustrations are either original drawings or from old engravings in possession of the author.